Eph. 2:10

Created for Purpose

The Inspirational Story of Northwest Medical Teams

Coffee House Publishers
32370 SE Judd Rd
Eagle Creek, Oregon 97022
888-896-4568

CREATED FOR PURPOSE

The Inspirational Story of Northwest Medical Teams

1999 by Ronald Post
ISBN: 0-9663176-6-1

For information:

Coffee House Publishers
32370 SE Judd Rd
Eagle Creek, Oregon 97022
888-896-4568

DEDICATION

This book is dedicated to my friend, my partner and my wife of forty years, Jean Post. She was there at the very birth of Northwest Medical Teams, International. She was by my side because she too wanted to do something to help the sick and dying Cambodians in 1979. Jean has always supported the vision I have of motivating people to use their time and resources to serve others in need. Through good times and bad, she worked untold hours to help establish this mission and few will ever know the level of commitment and work she put into this effort.

As this mission celebrates its 20th anniversary in 1999, I look back with awe at how Jean managed to work alongside this hard driving "A" personality. But she did and without her partnership, my work would have been more difficult. Every man or woman is blessed if they have a life partner who believes in, encourages, prays for, and helps them fulfill their life's dream and vision. I consider myself thus blessed.

CONTENTS

FOREWORD

In your hands you hold the story of the power of compassion and the drive that is created when a group of people team together to change a hurting world. This is a story that must be told. It is not a story about a great politician or a famous entertainer. It is a story of ordinary people accomplishing extraordinary things. But this story is more than that. It is a guidebook for anyone who has watched the evening news and felt a sense of hopelessness and a feeling that nothing can be done about the amount of pain and suffering in the world. It is for anyone who ever wondered, "what can I do? How can one person make a difference?" That is why *Created For Purpose* is an invigorating message of hope.

Ron Post has a soft heart and calloused hands. I first heard of him more than twenty years ago when he made a call to my office asking one of my staff if there was any need for medical relief in Cambodia. My staff member assured Mr. Post that there was and encouraged him to do anything he could; and we offered to help, as we were coordinating efforts of our own. We did not know at the time that Ron Post was just an ordinary man who had seen the evening news and was driven to do something about the situation. But people who are sure of God's calling in their lives are the most powerful people in this world. God had given Ron a vision and this man was going to take action.

This book tells the story of how one man decided to get up out of his chair and do something about hurting people. It is the story of how he got thousands more ordinary people to get out of their chairs and form teams that have impacted millions of lives. You cannot read this book without having a desire to do something. It will put a spark in your life and give you greater meaning and purpose.

What has happened over these last twenty years has been astonishing. It was my great pleasure to award Ron the Jefferson Award for his diligent work in feeding the hungry, healing the sick and sheltering the homeless. For me, Ron Post exemplifies the very heart of a caring and loving God. He is my friend, and it gives me great pleasure to introduce you to his story.

Northwest Medical Teams International is an organization of proactive people. Many of the doctors, nurses and non-medical work teams give their vacations year after year to stay in tents or shacks and care for people who the world has forgotten. You will clearly see why they do it over and over. They are heroes, each and every one. They remind us that the heart of man is still good.

My prayer is that this book will help guide you to God's plan and purpose for your life and prepare you for the rewards that come in helping your fellow man.

In an age of violence and unrest, *Created for Purpose* will reveal to you the wonderful promises involved in sacrificial living.

The Honorable Mark Hatfield
Former United States Senator, Oregon

CHAPTER ONE

WALKING INTO DARKNESS

Some wandered in desert wastelands, finding no way to a city
where they could settle. They were hungry and thirsty, and
their lives ebbed away. Psalm 107:4

The seven-acre compound was surrounded by barbed wire. Armed guards were posted around the camp, ready to shoot any refugee attempting escape. Crammed inside these seven acres were 40,000 people. I was born on seven acres in San Bernadino, California. How could an entire city of people fit into the place where I grew up?

These 40,000 unfortunates were eking out an existence on a diet of two spoonfuls of rice a day. The lack of sufficient nutrients caused their bodies to be susceptible to many diseases and sicknesses. They were without possessions, without homes, without a country, and it seemed as if many were without hope. They had escaped the dictator of their country, only to face hunger, sickness, and death.

Before we even reached the compound, we began to understand the consequences of so many people living in such a small place. The odor of the open trenches filled with human waste was overwhelming. I wanted to grab my handkerchief and hold it over my nose, and I felt the urge to vomit. I struggled, and willed that I would not do either. These people were suffering greatly; I could stand to suffer a little, also.

The camp gate swung open and our first volunteer medical team entered the compound. We looked out over a sea of depressed and dying people. They were all arrayed in black clothes that hung loosely on their thin and frail frames. Though the sun was shining, it failed to cheer the dismal sight before us. We were enveloped in darkness. I looked into the faces of these people as I walked with our team towards the hospital ward. Their eyes were as dark as the clothing they wore, and they stared blankly at nothing.

It was November, 1979. The place was Thailand, and the refugees were Cambodians. During the years of 1975-1979, thousands of Cambodians fled from their homes to escape the cruel dictator Pol Pot. These were the days of the "killing fields," a term made popular by the movie of the same name. In search of refuge, the Cambodians crossed over to Thailand. Hungry, sick, and disheartened by the loss of loved ones, many stumbled across the border, weakened by their sufferings, as if they were seeking a quiet place to die.

Now, here I stood among them, leading a medical team. This was something I had never done before. The team of physicians, nurses, and paramedics also had never been to a place like this before. Questions raced through my mind as I surveyed the scene before me. Did I do the right thing? Would the team accomplish the hard tasks ahead? After all, these medical volunteers would be treating diseases that they had never encountered. I wondered what the others were thinking and feeling. They were like me, Americans. Mass tragedies like this just didn't happen in America.

Our medical team had been assigned to a hospital ward by World Vision International, a Christian relief and development agency. We had been asked to run a 125-bed ward and also care for hundreds of outpatients. We weaved toward our assigned station; a long building with a thatched roof and gravel floors. An endless row of cots bedded more pain and anguish than I had ever seen.

The air was filled with the sounds of moaning. A young woman cried out in pain. Beside her lay her infant who was nearly dead. His skin stretched tightly over protruding bones. For the first time in my comfortable American life, I looked into the face of hunger.

The sick people lay there with pleading eyes, praying for

someone to help. A 15-year-old boy moaned. He had been through the stomach and the bullet had exited just above his rectum. Feces seeped from his body, and he could not find comfort for his pain.

Who was I that I should live in America? Why was I so blessed? We were created by God with the same needs, desires, and emotions. We all wanted to take care of our families, enjoy life and stay healthy. Yet, instead, the Cambodians had been denied the "pursuit of happiness" and had to struggle just to survive.

I looked at a sick man nearby. The difference between us was only our place of birth. Had I been born in Cambodia, I might be the one lying in a make-shift hospital ward praying for help. How often had I taken America for granted? I somehow believed that American citizenship was a deserved right. I thought we were a superior people, blessed because of the right choices we had made. How could I have ignored these oppressed and hurting people for so long? I had so much to learn and so many changes to make in my life.

What terrible sufferings! The stench, the wailing and groaning, the emaciated bodies fighting disease -- my senses were overwhelmed. Why me? I am a common person -- a businessman. I looked back on the events that brought me half way around the globe. How did this journey begin? How was this vision given to me? It did not come to me after days of fasting on a mountain top. Nor did it come while I was on my knees before the church altar. No, the story of God calling me to Cambodia is as strange as any story in the Old Testament. I felt out of place, confused and insufficient. I felt exactly the way God wanted me to feel.

My easy chair
The spirit is willing, but the body is weak. Matthew 26:41

It was not long ago that I was returning from my business office to my comfortable Salem, Oregon, home. The trees were beginning to cast away their golden garments, while we began piling on ours. Rains are common all year round, but November

...t drizzle, and today was no exception. I
...se, eager to wind down.
...ening, my wife and I watched the evening news
...again, the terrible scenes of the Cambodian
...before our eyes. Jean and I looked at each other,
dec...   by the pictures of suffering. We wished there was
someth...   ...e could do to help.

As we continued to watch, I saw a scene of aid workers picking up a body from a rice field. The body appeared to be a teenage girl who had probably starved to death. I glanced across the room and gazed at our teenage daughter, Sheri. She was sleeping sweetly on our couch. She was healthy and beautiful. Then, the pain hit. That could be my Sheri they were picking up from a rice field. How awful that a young girl with her girlish hopes and desires should be denied any chance to reach them. Her life had been cut short. Then I asked myself, "Why was I blessed to be born here and not there? I didn't choose to be born here. Nor did the parents of that Cambodian teenager choose to be born there!"

As I pondered that thought, a plan entered my mind as clearly as though someone had written it on paper and handed it to me. The plan was simple, but very precise: recruit a medical team and lead it to help the Cambodians in two weeks' time.

At first I argued with myself. How could I ever persuade the medical community to go? Why would they follow me? I had no medical background. I was a businessperson. What did I know of medical needs? Even if I could persuade medical personnel to go, how would I get them there in two weeks? What about supplies and the money it would take to ship them there?

Fearful of sharing this with Jean, I balked at first. However, a forceful conviction to do something caused me to blurt out my plan. Jean looked at me and said, "Yes! I didn't want to say anything, but I just knew we had to help these people."

Jean's confirmation helped my faith. I could not ignore the inspiration any longer. Those people needed help, and I knew I would have to get out of my easy chair and do something. We eagerly began brainstorming on how to accomplish what we believed was God's plan.

We needed more information. Jean and I supported two missionary friends, Marty and Jan Larson, in Thailand. Perhaps they could tell me if the need for medical people was urgent. I called the headquarters of Marty's and Jan's mission group, New Tribes, in Bangkok, Thailand. Marty and Jan were not available, but the director quickly informed me that the situation of the Cambodian refugees was critical. Many were dying from lack of medical care.

The urgency in his voice was contagious. I decided to call Don Clark, the news reporter from KEZI-TV in Eugene, Oregon, who had done the story we saw that evening. I had heard of Don because he was known as a Christian speaker around the Northwest. It was late that night when I called the station and asked if I could speak to him. To my surprise, they put me through.

Don later talked about that initial conversation: "Do you know how many weird calls we get at a station? Here it is midnight and this man is telling me he wants to raise up a medical team and go help the Cambodians! Yet, I listened to this man and sensed something real and special about his call. I said, 'Mr. Post, I don't know what I can do, but whatever you do, I will cover it.'"

Don also advised me to call Mike Donahue at KOIN-TV in Portland, and Senator Mark Hatfield, whom he believed would be more informed. Don would later become a close friend, serve on our board, and be the first television news person to cover our team in Thailand.

The media would be one of the key ingredients in the making of our mission. I quickly discovered that the media is made up of individuals who can be just as compassionate and called as any other citizens. Many reporters and camera people wanted to be part of this great movement. Reporter after reporter would go out with our teams over the years. They would perform their jobs as professionals, but behind the scenes, they would break down and cry over what they witnessed.

The next morning, I called Senator Hatfield's office in Washington, D.C. Though he was unavailable, I spoke to one of his assistants and explained my plan. He replied that Senator Hatfield had been in close contact with the situation and felt medical help was urgently needed. He asked if someone could call me later. I said "yes."

Later, the secretary of Dr. Stanley Mooneyham, President of World Vision, called. Dr. Mooneyham had been asked by the International component of World Vision to recruit a medical team for a field hospital ward at a refugee camp in Thailand. At that stage of World Vision's growth, they had never recruited medical teams before.

The secretary asked, "Mr. Post, can you recruit medical teams?"

I answered without thinking, Yes!

She said, "Good! We will be sending a representative to Portland to meet with you."

I hung up the phone, sat down, astonished at what had just happened. Then, I prayed.

"Lord, you gave me this plan. I know you did, but what do I do now?"

Feelings of insufficiency welled up inside me. World Vision was a big international relief agency. They surely would have more means than me to recruit medical teams. Why me? I had no experience internationally. What about all those questions I had been bombarded with when I was first given this plan? None of them was answered. Instead, I had more pressure to accomplish the impossible, now that World Vision was counting on me. Inwardly, I groaned. Oh, why did I blurt "yes" out so quickly? I sighed and realized I had passed the point of no return. Then, I felt as if my spirit was squaring its shoulders and urging me to trust God, work hard, and see what happened.

Knee-deep in Impossibilities
For nothing is impossible with God. Luke 1:37

I asked a pastor friend if he knew of any missionary doctors from whom I could seek out advice. He gave me the names of two former missionary doctors living in Portland. I called them and explained my vision. They agreed to meet me at the Hill Villa, a restaurant in Portland at noon. For support, I asked Jean and my personal physician, Dr. Earl Van Volkinburg, to accompany me on the 45 mile trip.

Taking Don Clark's advice, I placed a call to Mike Donahue from KOIN-TV. I was once again surprised to be put right through to Mike. He patiently listened to my story.

When I was finished, Mike said, "Ron, why don't you let all of the television, radio stations, and newspapers know about your meeting tomorrow?" Unfamiliar with the protocol of a press conference, I followed Mike's suggestion and called for one. I was not expecting anyone from the media to actually show. If I had been, it would have made me very nervous.

The next morning, I was eager to get to the meeting so I decided to leave early. Jean and Dr. Van Volkinburg would drive together and arrive later. Others expected to attend the luncheon

were the two missionary doctors and the World Vision representative.

I pulled into the restaurant and parked the car. As I walked into the front doors, two very agitated missionary doctors confronted me.

"What is going on here?" one asked.

"What do you mean?" I said.

Ron Post with Portland news anchorman, Mike Donahue.

"What I mean is the room is full of reporters! We believed this was an informational meeting with you. We didn't know you were bringing reporters."

My stomach tightened. I should have informed these doctors. I apologized, but they returned to the room obviously upset.

I paused to pray, "Lord, help me get through this."

I walked into the room where the lunch was to take place. I was blinded by the lights from the television camera. My heart raced. This crazy plan was going to air on television. I felt panicky, but had enough wits about me to seat everyone. I sat at one end of the long table. When Jean and Dr. Van Volkinburg arrived, they sat at the other end near the door. How I longed to sit beside them, partly because I desperately needed their moral support, and partly because it was near the door!

We broke the ice by chatting about the situation in Cambodia. Though the conversation was polite, the hard, cold looks from the doctors continually reminded me that, for now, I was in hostile territory. And all the while, the cameras rolled.

Finally, one of the doctors asked me to explain my plan. I told them the plan just as it had been given to me -- recruit a medical team and take this team in two weeks to Thailand. When, I finished, I experienced one of those very long moments in which a second seems to be hours. I looked around expectantly, waiting for comments.

The first doctor said, "Well, you could never expect to have a team ready to go in two weeks. It would take several months to put something like this together."

The second doctor joined in and said, "I agree. You cannot expect doctors to leave their practices and nurses to get time off that soon. It will take months."

I was ready to crawl under the table. The mood in the room was subdued. How could things go so wrong? I had felt strongly about doing this. The doubts began to assail me from all sides. Did I really hear this call? Were the doctors right? It did seem like an impossible challenge. Those unanswered questions came back again, like phantoms refusing to leave an old haunt. How was I going to get people to volunteer that soon? What about the supplies they would need? Where would the finances come from? I felt as if my boat had sprung multiple leaks, and I was preparing to sink.

In my heart, I uttered a prayer, "Lord, I really felt you wanted me to do this. Please Lord, help me!"

When I finished this silent prayer, my friend Dr. Van Volkinburg raised his hand and from the other end of the table asked me a question.

"Ron, if a doctor called you, what is the first thing you would ask?"

"How soon can you go?" I replied, meaning that is the first question I would ask.   Dr. Van Volkinburg answered, "Oh, I could go in two weeks."

I asked, "Earl, are you volunteering?"

He said, "Yes!"

With enthusiasm in my voice, I said, "Great! You're my first volunteer."

Dr. Van Volkinburg's response to my question proved to be the pivotal point in getting a medical team to Thailand. Suddenly, the wall of impossibilities vanished and we could all see through God's eyes, "all things are possible." The entire mood at the luncheon changed.   The doctors agreed the plan could be accomplished, and the meeting adjourned with all members smiling. My plan was still floating, in spite of the shark-like doubts attacking it.

As soon as the meeting ended, reporters began firing questions at me. Yet, I felt confident that this plan was not my own invention, and its fate was in greater hands.   One reporter asked me, "Do you really believe you can assemble a team and arrive in Thailand in two weeks?

I questioned back, "Do you believe in God?"

She answered, "Yes."

"I do too, and if God wants us to be there in two weeks, we will be!" She later added that quote in her story.

God was in the process of teaching me something very important: Hold on to what you believe in your heart.   Stand firm! I now understood that He was in control of what happened. I just needed to be available and to pray that others would make themselves available as well. I would soon find out that I was just one part of a grand scheme that God had created.

They were waiting

Ask the Lord of the harvest, therefore, to send out workers into his harvest field. Matthew 9:38

Before I left the press conference, one of the television reporters said, "Ron, if you give us a telephone number before tonight's broadcast, we will be happy to display it so people will know where they can respond. In fact, I am sure the other stations would do the same."

For a moment, I thought about that comment. My home number only had one line on which we could be reached, and it would be long distance, being a Salem number. Would people call long distance? Ideally, we should have toll-free lines. However, I was in Portland, 45 miles from home, and it was now 1:30 p.m. The news would air at 6:00 p.m. I had only four and a half hours to make the ideal happen.

I rushed back to Salem, and immediately called a friend, Reg Farnsworth, who had converted a house on Market Street into an office. By the time we had ended our conversation, he had agreed to let us use a room in his building.

Another friend with whom I attended church worked with the phone company. I called, and asked, "Woody, could you get your company to donate two toll-free lines?" Woody replied, "Yes, I think so, Ron. However it will take about two weeks."

"Two weeks?" I said, incredulous.

He asked, "Well, how soon did you need them, Ron?"

"Tonight!" I replied, decisively.

The pain in Woody's voice was evident when he answered, "What? I can't do that!"

I said, "Woody, that is when I need it. Would you do what you can?"

An hour later, Woody called me back. "Ron, we can do it!"

He gave me the telephone numbers they would be assigning, and I immediately called the television, radio stations, and newspapers.

Within two hours of arriving in Salem, an office had been

secured, and two toll-free lines had been donated. This was something that was seemingly impossible to man. Yet, everything was falling into place. Each step of the way, God was showing me that HE was working everything out, and all I had to do was be His voice in asking.

Asking for things like this was not what I had been accustomed to doing. In the past, I would either do it myself or pay to have it done. Now, I found myself dependent on others to help me. I began to understand Paul's description of the body of Christ in which each member is dependent on the others. This was not my project. It was God's. We were all just involving ourselves in God's plan.

It was 5:30 p.m. Jean and I had set up a long table in our borrowed office, and two telephones were sitting in front of us. We had brought a television with us to watch the news.

I was nervous! Would the media air the story? Would anyone call? Did others feel the way we did? In about a half hour, we would know. At six o'clock the news came on, and my heart began racing. Only a few minutes into the news, they reported, "A Salem man is trying to assemble a volunteer medical team and travel to the Cambodian refugee camps in Thailand."

The news anchor said, "Here is the number you can call for information."

The number appeared on the screen. Jean and I looked at each other in surprise, because both phones started ringing!

"Hi, I am a doctor and would like to know how I can volunteer."

"Hello. I want to donate money for the team to go."

"Hi, my name is Rick Stein. I'm an attorney. I'm willing to come down and empty wastebaskets if it would help."

"Hi, my name is Ed Cameron. I am a real estate agent. What can I do?"

Jean and I no sooner hung up the phone than it would ring again. It rang continuously all evening. They even ran the story on the 11 o'clock news and it rang even more. The phone rang until 1 a.m. We were amazed at the response we were getting. It was as though the Holy Spirit had whispered into the ears of hundreds of people who were just waiting for the opportunity to respond.

The telephone continued ringing day and night for two weeks. Medical people volunteered. Others volunteered to help answer phones or whatever else we needed. Many provided funds. In just two weeks, people sent in over $250,000! We were so thankful.

The media played a vital role in making this mission a success. For the first time in history, the media was reporting live about the refugees. We had seen the Viet Nam war on television news, but we had never seen the mass suffering of civilians. It was shocking to all of us. Now, the media was covering the preparations we were making to send our first team. Every day the television, radio, and newspaper reporters would be at our small borrowed office asking about our progress. The coverage kept people of the Northwest informed and involved.

Team Work
... in Christ we who are many form one body, and each member belongs to all the others. Matthew 12:5

We had so many wonderful volunteers for this mission. There were people to help with the large decisions such as selecting the medical team, and the small details such as answering telephones and filing. The nice thing about volunteers is that there are no jealousies and jockeying for position. All the workers were willing to help where help was needed.

We selected a medical team of twenty-eight people. After the selection process, we needed to acquire the necessary immunizations, passports, and visas. Again, an impossibility mounted before us -- it would take at least two weeks to get passports and visas. Yet, this time, I was confident that nothing was going to intimidate the originator of this plan -- God. I knew this team was to leave in two weeks. The doubts were gone.

Normal channels would never give us enough time to get the team passports and visas. That's when the workers began to get busy. Ed Cameron drove to Seattle, Washington, to walk the passport applications through for the team. Rick Stein jumped on a plane to Los Angeles on Thanksgiving Day to walk the visa applications through the Thailand Embassy. He camped on the embassy doorstep until they opened the next morning, and informed them he would wait there until the visas were approved. Rick and Ed would be important to our mission for years to come. Both would later serve on our board of directors.

There were many more who volunteered hours to help get that first team in the air to Thailand. Though I cannot recall all the names, I will always be grateful to those who responded. It seemed they were just waiting for someone to say, "Let's do it!" I was blessed by God to say those words, but if I had not responded, He would have chosen someone else to do it, because people were so ready.

All those questions I was so concerned about earlier were answered. How would I recruit the team, get the supplies, raise the money; and who would help? It all happened because I listened to that quiet voice, and acted on it. The rest simply unfolded.

Team work would become the very backbone of this mission. We were bonded by the single goal of helping people live. The volunteer in the office, the one donating funds, or the individuals that would go, were all part of a team. Like strands of rope woven together, people from all backgrounds joined to make this mission work.

The mission trip to Thailand was a grassroots effort and we wanted everyone in the Northwest to feel a part of it. Thus, our efforts came to be called Northwest Medical Teams. The name was officially selected within days of my getting the call to form this team of volunteers. Like everything else, the name just fell into place.

Fearing Failure

I can do everything through him who gives me strength. Philippians 4:13

Passports and visas were obtained. Medical volunteers had received their immunizations. We were just days away from departure. Though there were no doubts of whether we would arrive in Thailand, there were plenty of them about what would happen when we arrived there. I had never been to that part of the world in my life, and I was anxious. Concerns darted through my mind and unsettled my peace like mosquitoes unsettle a lovely outdoor evening. Would this team truly be valuable in saving lives? Would the Cambodians receive us as people wanting to help? I become nauseated at the sight of blood, and people who were really hurting would make me desperately sad. Would I be able to stomach what I was going to see in those camps?

The questions continued. Would there really be a place for the team to work and enough work to keep them busy? We brought together a team of twenty-eight people. Would they work as a team? We also would have media along on the trip. The Oregonian newspaper sent Julie Trip. The television station in Eugene, KEZI-TV, sent Don Clark with a cameraman, and a television station in Portland, KATU-TV, sent Stan Wilson with a cameraman. I was concerned about the stories they would share with people at home.

Time passed quickly, and it was the evening before our departure. Jean helped me pack. Secretly, she wrote little love notes and each one was rolled up in a pair of underwear. I was grateful for this while I was in Thailand, for each day I would look forward to a new note that contained an encouraging message. It kept me connected with her.

It was very difficult to sleep the night before we departed. I couldn't believe the obstacles that no longer existed. In two weeks time, the impossible had been made a reality. Yet, despite the miracles I had seen, I was still anxious about the events to come. Perhaps it is because if things went wrong, people wouldn't blame God, they'd blame me. Later, I would learn how to give more of my concerns to God.

Oregon's governor, Victor Atiyeh, and Washington's governor, Dixie Lee Ray, would attend our departure at the airport in the morning. Before we left, the team and their families would breakfast at a hotel by the Portland Airport at 5 a.m. We were to be joined by Governor Atiyeh. This would be the first time the team would meet each other.

The next morning we were on our way up the freeway again, heading toward the breakfast meeting. It was a wonderful experience getting to know each team member and their families. Governor Atiyeh spoke words of encouragement to the team. Before the team left for the airport, he joined with us in a circle to pray for God's protection and to ask Him to use the team in a mighty way. Later, there were a lot of tearful good-byes from family members as we began to board the plane.

A feeling of awe came over me as I watched each member say good-bye and walk down the tunnel. Were we about to accomplish the plan God had whispered to me while watching the evening news just two short weeks ago? Yes We had done it! God had His perfect will fulfilled in us. In a few days, we would be heading through the bamboo and grass to the field hospital ward where our ministry would truly begin.

We entered into that hospital ward and experienced those heart-wrenching moments when the pain surrounding us was almost overwhelming. Then, our team got to work, and all my questions and concerns disappeared. Though this team of medical volunteers had never worked together before, nor treated tropical diseases, they courageously set about their tasks with a vigor that warmed my heart. Their excellent training was evident. The team leader, Dr. Bruce Flaming, gathered the team, and they quickly formulated a plan to care for the 125-patient ward. Assignments were made, and they began checking each patient and getting a history. It was obvious that they were in their element.

While in route to Thailand, I heard many members of the team questioning among themselves. They were asking questions like, "What illnesses will we see? What kind and how many medicines will we have? What diagnostic equipment will be available?" I could sense they did not know what to expect. They knew there were illnesses and parasites they had never treated. However, the questions vanished the moment they walked into that hospital ward. It's like a preacher walking into his pulpit. Each knew where he or she belonged. It was a joy to watch.

I was reminded of a story about a boy who was walking with his family on the beach. They were surrounded by millions of shelled creatures that had washed to the shore, and would die without water. The boy kept picking up the shells, and throwing them back into the water. His family, impatient with his slow progress, turned to him and said, "Will you stop throwing those things? What difference will it make?" The boy picked up a shell, and threw it in the water. "It makes a difference to that one," he replied, and kept throwing.

Many people were very sick and in great pain. I thought it had to be difficult for our volunteers to deal with so many hurting people, and I assumed they would become overwhelmed by the task. However, I underestimated the team. Each began helping one person at a time, and each would make a huge difference, one life at a time.

Laughter is Universal
A cheerful heart is good medicine... Proverbs 17:22

One morning, as I walked into our hospital ward, I noticed our news reporter, Don Clark, playing a guitar for the children. They seemed very excited and were laughing. The laughter caught my attention because, in the midst of such misery, any kind of happiness was lacking. Their lives had been shattered and their world had been torn apart. Why should they laugh? Yet, when I saw how much these children loved Don's playing, I had an idea.

A huge pile of wood was stacked up for cooking fires in the compound. It must have been twenty feet high. I suggested to Don that he get up on that wood pile and sing to the people. I said that it might brighten them up and, hopefully, bring a smile to their faces. Don agreed, but told me I would have to join him. We climbed up about ten feet on the wood pile.

Don and I started singing every song we could remember. At first, a few curious people stopped to hear us. They were joined by more and more every minute, until there were several thousand people watching us. They stood there with somber faces. We were running out of songs.

Finally, I asked Don, "Do you remember that old song, *The Wayward Wind?*"

Don said, "Yes, I do."

"You start singing it, and I will join in on the chorus," I said.

While Don was singing a verse, I pretended as if I was riding a horse and bouncing to the tune. I had a baseball hat on and when Don got to the chorus I spun the cap around backwards, mimicked a cross-eyed contorted look and blurted out as loudly as I could, "BUT----the wayward wind!"

Everyone jumped! It seemed as if they had all been jolted by a cattle prod. For a moment, I thought I might have done something wrong. Then, we heard it. From across that sea of people came an almost silent ripple of laughter. It began to swell and build. It was a laughter that came from the depths of their being. Stored up for nearly three years, the misery they had bottled up began to pour out of them. Now, an army could not hold back the emotion.

Even though they could not understand the language, they could sense the meaning. Whenever Don would sing the verse, I would go back to riding the horse. We noticed they were anticipating the chorus, so I did not disappoint them. I hit the word "BUT" harder than before. Don and I would never forget this experience. As much as food and medicine were needed for their bodies, laughter was needed for their souls.

Don told me later how someone caught his attention as he looked to the very back of the huge crowd. There stood an old nun in her white habit with her hands raised towards heaven, the tears flowing from her eyes. As we sang the final song, "Kum-ba yah, my Lord" (Come by here, my Lord), Don sensed that the nun was praying the words for her people who needed a heavenly touch -- one that could only be provided by "My Lord."

NEW BEGINNINGS
...he restores my soul. Psalm 23:3

A young Cambodian girl had arrived in the camp quite ill and near death. She was admitted to the Northwest Medical Teams ward where Dr. Phyllis Cavens cared for her until she recovered. It then came time for the young woman to return from the ward back into the camp. At the time of the discharge, the young lady began to weep heavily and pleaded with Phyllis not to put her back in the camp. When Phyllis asked why, the young girl told her story.

Mai was the daughter of a couple who had a successful book store in Cambodia. The ruthless Communist dictator, Pol Pot, came into power and began to "cleanse" the country by eliminating western influences. He took this to the extreme by executing anyone who was educated. Many teachers, doctors, business people and other professionals died during this period. Some were executed just for wearing eyeglasses.

One day Mai saw Khmer Rouge soldiers come to her father's bookstore. They executed her father and mother in front of her. She was then dragged from her home by the soldiers and forced to work and serve as a sex slave. She had to travel with the soldiers while living on a starvation diet. When the Vietnamese invaded Cambodia, these soldiers had to flee through the jungle. She was dragged for days. Finally, when they came close to the Thai border, she escaped and stumbled into the refugee camp. Phyllis found her near starvation.

When Mai finished her story, she said, "Dr. Phyllis if you send me back into the camp, these same soldiers will rape me again!"

Dr. Phyllis gave her a job in the hospital ward so she would not have to return. When Phyllis was due to rotate home, Mai came to her. Mai wrapped her arms around Phyllis and said, "Thank you. You are my new beginning!"

The first time I heard Phyllis relay this story, I was filled with joy. Our teams gave "new beginnings" for hundreds of Cambodians. The teenage girl they picked up out of a rice field that I had seen on television couldn't be helped. She died. However, just to know Dr. Phyllis and the team saved this one young woman's life made everything worthwhile. A life is priceless.

Dr. Phyllis Cavens standing with the girl she gave "new beginnings" to in a Cambodian Refugee Camp in 1979. Phyllis was on the first Northwest Medical Teams Intl team. She and her husband, Dr. Travis Cavens, have since been nearly everywhere Northwest Medical Teams Intl has responded to crisis. Photo courtesy of Dr. Phyllis Cavens.

When our team had arrived we were faced with the grim report that thirty to forty people each day were dying in the camp. However, during the entire time our team operated the field hospital ward in Sa Keao Refugee camp, not one patient died!

I returned from Thailand, believing this was a one time thing. Jean and I were just excited that God had used us to help the Cambodians. My next plan was to go back to my business practice and make a living. Little did I know that we would be part of giving "new beginnings" to millions of people over the next twenty years.

CHAPTER TWO

THE WAR WITHIN

*Then Jesus said to his disciples, "If anyone would come after me, he must
deny himself and take up his cross and follow me. For whoever wants to
save his life will lose it, but whoever loses his life for me will find it."*
Matthew 16:24,25

I returned from Thailand with a heavy heart and a high
fever. A tropical illness had infected my body, and for days my
temperature wavered around 104 degrees Fahrenheit. During
that time I would often break down and cry. The images in those
camps haunted me. The evils of what one can do to a fellow
human being are horrible.

Northwest Medical Teams continued to rotate to Thailand

Part of the first vol-
unteer team in
1979 celebrates
Christmas with
Thai workers out-
side a Cambodian
refugee camp.
Photo courtesy of
NWMT.

over a six-month period until the conditions got better for the
Cambodians. All those involved in the Thailand mission felt a
deep satisfaction in the work that was accomplished. I felt good
about answering God's call. Now, the situation was improved,
and it was time to get back to business.

For fifteen years, I had been a successful entrepreneur. My
system would be to start a business or buy a business that need-

ed help. Once the business was built up and successful, I would sell it. The hats I had worn throughout my working life were numerous. I had operated a catering truck business, a large general engineering company, a radio station, a manufacturing business, retail stores, restaurants, a distributor business, and many other enterprises.

Working hard is a character trait in my family, began by my father. Raising a family during the Great Depression, W.B. (Bill) Post's drive and perseverance impressed my siblings and me. Papa was a motor grader operator most of his adult life, and he could work that grader like a master sculptor can work clay. He achieved excellence because he loved what he did and he worked hard doing it. His unending pursuit of excellence made him the best. Papa always told us to be the best at what we do and to work harder than anyone else.

I followed my father's example. Working hard, pursuing excellence, and doing my best were all part of my daily routine. The American dream sat in the palm of my hand, and all I had to do was fold my fingers over it and grasp it for my own. Yet, all the while, a battle raged inside me, and I kept my hand open, waiting for something more.

Several years passed and my thoughts would often wander back to Thailand and the people we helped. I tried to guess where their paths had led. My mind had etched certain scenes into my heart, and I would often visit them there. There was the portrait of Nurse Teresa Brisbin, sitting on a cot, holding a 20-pound, five-year-old boy, Lon. The team brought him back from starvation and illness. There was such a joy in our hearts when we knew he would survive.

Memory brought back a young father who was ill and was losing ground each day. Dr. Cavens and Dr. Frisbie fought hard to save this man, but our efforts seemed futile. One day, I asked Dr. Cavens if he would live. She said, "I can't do anything else for him." I knelt by this man's bedside and placed my hand on his body and prayed for the Lord to heal him. Dr. Cavens also prayed. We were elated when our prayers were answered and the man lived!

When I shared these stories with friends, they would often say, "Ron, just think about this. What if you had not gotten out of your chair that night and moved to action? Would these people be alive today?" That question mulled around in my brain.

I tried to keep my mind on my business interests, but I couldn't. The fulfillment had been stripped away. Spending my time making money just didn't make sense. How could it when I had witnessed such tragic events and had played a part in changing them? Yet, it was a family tradition to make money, and I felt pressured to follow it. Several in my family were already close to becoming millionaires. "Maybe after I make mine, I could do more about helping people," I thought. Yet, the scriptures would often remind me of our need to care for the poor, and I would feel convicted. Striking a balance between my profession, which gives me the means to live, and following God's word, which speaks about spending ourselves on behalf of the poor, was going to be difficult.

In 1984, powerful feelings about Northwest Medical Teams welled up inside me. The conviction to form Northwest Medical Teams as a permanent mission could no longer be pushed aside. Ideas spilled from my mind as if I had been planning the mission for years. The goal would be the same: recruit medical teams. However, the time would be indefinite and the place was the globe. We would travel around the world helping people live!

Though the conviction was strong, these thoughts collided with my upbringing. My family had taught me well and had given me strong ideals by which to live: work hard to give my family things they could enjoy, and secure my retirement. These were wise and lofty goals. However, I could not escape these feelings about Northwest Medical Teams. Events were about to happen to bring this struggle to an end, and they would come from a place I never suspected.

Priorities

Love the Lord your God ... Love your neighbor as yourself. Mark 12:30,31

Little did I know that across the country two men were discussing the issues that were causing the struggles within my heart. My news anchor friend, Don Clark, who had accompanied me to Thailand, had been speaking with Doug Coe from the Fellowship group in Washington, DC, about his experiences with the Cambodians in 1979. Doug was an Oregonian and a close friend of Senator Mark Hatfield; they had attended college together and were both members of the Fellowship. The Fellowship was instrumental in putting on the Presidential prayer breakfast and the governors' prayer breakfasts in each state.

Don shared how many lives had been saved and the great response from the people of the Northwest. When Doug heard some of the stories, it moved him. With tears in his eyes, Doug reached across the table and grabbed Don's hands. His voice broke as he asked, "Why has the mission stopped?"

Don replied, "I do not know why, Doug, but I will ask Ron Post."

The telephone rang. It was Don. It had been months since I had spoken with him. "I wanted to ask you," he said, "why Northwest Medical Teams hasn't continued its work?"

"Don this gives me goose bumps," I answered. I explained the struggles that I had been experiencing, and the issues with which I had wrestled. I also shared my conviction to establish Northwest Medical Teams as a permanent mission.

"Don, I haven't known what to do with these thoughts, but I've wondered if they were planted by God's Holy Spirit. Strangely enough, several other friends have called me, seemingly out of the blue, to ask if I had ever thought of forming NWMT as a permanent mission. It has been three years. It's hard for me to understand why this would be happening now. The answer is not clear at all."

Don asked, "Ron would you mind if I spoke to Doug Coe again?"

"Not at all," I said. "I really want the mind of Christ in this and if Doug has any helpful suggestions, great."

Later, I received a telephone call from a future lifetime friend. Bruce Sundberg, from the Fellowship, called to invite me to Washington, DC, and share my story with the group.

Each day while in Washington, I had the opportunity to tell my story to a number of people. The responses I received were very encouraging, and helped to confirm that the Fellowship supported what I was doing.

On the last evening before I returned to Oregon, Bruce Sundberg took me to Doug's house. Doug greeted us at the door and upon entering, he immediately said, "Let's see how good you are at darts."

An uneasiness came over me. It was as if I had been moving along at a smooth and quick pace, with everyone waving and smiling at me as I passed by, and someone had shifted down. That uncomfortable whine of my engine was unexpected. This was not the reason why I had come. Unnerved, I had a hard time even hitting the dart board. However, after the game, we sat down and Doug asked me to share my story. After telling him how God had called me in 1979, I told him about this strong feeling I had to form Northwest Medical Teams as a permanent mission.

Doug responded with a question, "What are God's priorities for your life?" Again, his approach caused me to feel uneasy.

"To love God." I said.

"What else?" Doug asked.

"Well, I guess to love my neighbor," I said. I was wondering where this was leading.

Doug picked up a Bible and began to read from Mark 12:28-31. "One of the teachers of the law came and heard them debating. Noticing that Jesus had given them a good answer, he asked him, 'Of all the commandments, which is the most important?' 'The most important one,' answered Jesus, 'is this: Hear, O Israel, the Lord our God, the Lord is one. Love the Lord your God with all your heart and with all your soul and with all your mind and with all your strength. The second is this, love your neighbors as yourself. There is no commandment greater than these.'"

When Doug finished reading these passages he said, "Ron, who is your closest neighbor?"

I thought for a minute and said, "I guess my family is my closest neighbor."

"That's right," Doug nodded, and added. "It didn't say anything about a mission or your job, did it?" Then, he said, "Here is what you should do. Go back to Oregon and form a support group who will hold you accountable to the priorities to which God has called us. That is to love the Lord and your family. Let that support group begin to pray with you about what the Lord wants to do with this mission. If you do this, we will pray for you and give you what help we can. If you do not do this, good luck, because that's all I will offer you."

After leaving Doug's house I had to wonder what steamroller had just flattened me! I expected Doug to give me an affirmation of what I planned to do. Being a "just do it" sort of guy, that is what I had in store for NWMT — I was just going to do it. Instead, I received a check that caused all sorts of doubts. Doug told me not to worry about the mission — just pray, form a support group, and concentrate on my priorities. For a person of action, this was not welcome advice. Yet, I did not discount what he had said.

Later, I would come to know Doug better. He is a person who believes with all his heart that God has called each of us to live by the priority Jesus established in scripture. He adheres to those words and has a support group that holds him accountable. Doug is simply a person who is going to get right to the heart of what he believes.

Inadequacies
Oh Lord, please send someone else to do it. Exodus 4:13

I returned with Bruce Sundberg to his house with many things swirling through my head. We sat in his house chatting about the evening and about the many people I had met that week while visiting the Fellowship.

Suddenly, I broke into uncontrollable sobbing. My emotions were completely beyond my control. Bruce must have sat in shock as I cried harder than I could ever remember doing before. He sat there, quietly waiting.

The sobs lessened, and a calm came over me for a moment. Yet, another emotion siezed me — a great sense of fear.

I shouted, "I am not the one to do this! I am not a doctor! I am not a good speaker! I do not have a degree! Someone else should do this! It should be a doctor or someone else who has more talents and abilities. I am not qualified!"

Sharing this conviction with all these great men had exposed me to much pressure. The responsibilities of forming a permanent mission was overwhelming. This would not be a crazy adventure for two weeks, a temporary dive into compassion. No, this would be my life's career. Compassion as a career was not security. In the world's eyes, it was not even wise. On the contrary, it seemed dangerous and risky.

The questions again surrounded me. I felt as if I were in a dark room with a bright light shining on me, and I was being interrogated. Would people support it? How would I support my family? What if I failed? I was wrestling with Doug's words. "Don't worry about the mission. Form a support group. Maintain God's priorities for your life, and pray." These were simple instructions, but they required a release of control, and turning over everything to God. I realized that this endeavor would be too big for my efforts. I was going to have to make a step of faith from which there was no retreat.

Bruce allowed my feelings to spin out of me. When I was calm, he said, "Ron, let's pray and go to bed."

Shame spread over me. I had just spilled my guts to this man. I had made myself completely transparent, allowing him to witness one of the most emotional experiences of my life and all he could say was, "Ron, let's pray and go to bed?" He was not offering me a solution, like I had hoped. Once I went to bed, the problem would still be lurking in my mind. Perhaps I was looking for Bruce to offer me a way out — to shift the responsibility from my shoulders by telling me the anguish was unnecessary and to carry on with my life as before. However, he didn't, and later, I was grateful he didn't.

Bruce may have slept well that night, but I did not. The next morning, I came downstairs and joined Bruce for breakfast on his deck. It was a beautiful spring day in the capitol. I felt awkward and confused.

Bruce's Bible lay next to his plate. When breakfast was finished, he broke the quietude that had hovered over us. "Ron, I was praying this morning and I believe the Lord gave me a word for you."

He picked up his Bible and began to read Joshua 1:5-9. After forty years in the desert, God finally allowed the Israelites to enter the promised land. God gave specific instructions and promises to Joshua for leading His people into the land of Caanan. Bruce read aloud, "No one will be able to stand up against you all the days of your life. As I was with Moses, so I will be with you; I will never leave you nor forsake you. Be strong and courageous, because you will lead these people to inherit the land I swore to their forefathers to give them. Be strong and very courageous. Be careful to obey all the law my servant Moses gave you; do not turn from it to the right or to the left, that you may be successful wherever you go. Do not let this Book of the Law depart from your mouth; meditate on it day and night, so that you may be careful to do everything written in it. Then you will be prosperous and successful. Have I not commanded you? Be strong and courageous. Do not be terrified; do not be discouraged, for the Lord your God will be with you wherever you go."

My spirit soared. It felt like a holiday with rockets exploding in the air! As Bruce read, it was as though God was speaking directly to me! The pressure was lifted from my back. The annointment of the Holy Spirit poured over me. I felt power fill my body. In these passages, God had answered all my concerns. The anxiety was gone. I was given the faith to believe that the mission would be supported and I would be able to support my family. The inadequacies fled. I could return home with a heart that was anticipating the work of God. Doug's suggestion to gather a support group around me and allow the Lord to guide us would be my next step.

When I returned to Oregon and explained to Jean all that had occurred, Jean had a good idea. "Let's call some of the busiest people in Salem and ask them to be our support group for prayer and accountability."

We began calling people like Rick and Clover Stein, Ed and Barb Cameron, and others who had helped us in the beginning. We called Dave and Jo Adams, Don and Delores Wyant, Eleanor Pearson, Buck and Diane Windom, and Phil and Nancy Nash. All these people were busy in their professions. Each was very involved in their churches. Yet, to our amazement, everyone said "yes" to our request.

Each week, our living room would be filled with these wonderful disciples. The agenda was simple: devotions and prayer. Seeking for an answer to what God wanted us to do was an interesting experience. Patience was slowly working its way into our character. For seven months, we gathered to seek direction from the Lord.

One evening, in October of 1984, I was once again watching the evening news from my easy chair. The news reporter announced, "A tragedy of immense proportion has befallen the country of Ethiopia. It is shocking."

The images from the television screen leapt out, and I felt as if I were there among these suffering people. Starving and emaciated bodies of children and elderly people staggered across the view of the camera. Long lines of men carried bodies to be buried. Thousands of sick and dying people struggled to reach a feeding center, and thousands died along the roads trying. The terrible drought had been compounded by the civil war to oust the Communist regime. Millions of people were starving, and hundreds of thousands were expected to die.

I recalled the images of the Cambodians I saw on television news back in 1979, but it did not compare with the multitude of people I was now seeing. The massive tragedy dwarfed the troubles of the Cambodian refugees. My heart ached, and I cried over the suffering I was watching. It became clear to me why our support group was meeting. God had been preparing us for this moment. He spent seven months shaping our hearts and building our strength, so we could minister to these people.

Our support group gathered together, and all agreed we should recruit medical teams to help the Ethiopians. Since we had worked with World Vision International before, I immediately called one of their representatives. He informed me that they were operating seven health and feeding centers in Ethiopia, but lacked medical care. They asked whether we could provide medical teams for each of their centers. Once again, I said yes to the calling. However, this time, with the preparation supporting me, I said it with confidence.

Our group knew this was going to be a permanent mission. We all were striving to accomplish our vision of recruiting volunteer teams to go anywhere in the world and express the love of Christ by rendering aid to the helpless. Souls would be restored as they were in Cambodia. The poorest of the poor would be reached. Like the young Cambodian woman who was helped by Dr. Phyllis Cavens, there would be many more "new beginnings."

Organizational details needed to be attended to. We needed to be accepted as a non-profit organization. Rick Stein, an attorney, quickly began to make calls to this end. Our next immediate need would be an office where volunteers could help put the teams together. Don Wyant said, "I might have something for us."

Later, he took me to his office building. Don asked, "Would this do?"

I exclaimed, "Don, there must be 1500 square feet here!"

"That's right," he said.

"How could you donate this much space?" I questioned, aloud. I will never forget Don's response. With tears welling up in his eyes, he said, "Whatever I have belongs to the Lord and if He needs this space, it is my privilege to give it." He even gave us the use of all the desks and chairs we would need.

Don Wyant would be the first of many people who would open his pocketbook to give money or make material items available to the mission. The grassroots efforts that was the foundation of Northwest Medical Teams had begun.

Accountability would be important to maintain a sound

standing with those who would support this mission. Early on, we joined a national group called Evangelical Council For Financial Accountability (ECFA). Its motto is, "Accountable to God and man." To belong to this group, each organization must meet many standards including an annual audit by an independent auditor, which is made available to the public.

The media of the Northwest once again helped to inform and involve people. Reporters covered our story on television and in the newspapers every day for weeks. Medical and office volunteers started calling in to offer help. Soon, our office was bustling with activity. Eager workers came and participated in big and small ways with a single goal as our focus: sending a medical team to Ethiopia.

As I analyzed the events that led me to form this permanent mission, I believe that my experience with the Fellowship in Washington, DC, was a pivotal point. When I decided to follow Doug's directions, which I now believe were inspired by God, I humbled myself to doing good in God's way and timing, not my own.

I tend to be a very impulsive person. I see a need and I want to fill it, immediately. Waiting seven months for the Lord to give me direction was not something I was accustomed to doing. Yet our group formed a very special relationship with each other and with the Lord, that can only be accomplished over time. Our commitment deepened and enabled us to see the mission flourish. Meeting together helped me stay accountable to the priorities the Lord had given us. I learned an important lesson. Even today, I meet every week with a group of men who hold me accountable.

In forming this mission, I was seeking purpose for my life. I would find it by helping others. A life without purpose is empty. My life was about to be filled with more riches than all the money in the world, and I would find it in the midst of immense suffering. Intense hunger, sickness, and pain would become my life's work and burden. I was going to come face to face with my Jesus, who would look at me through the eyes of "the least of these" (Matthew 25).

After deciding that this would be my purpose, God was

about to thrust me into the greatest area of suffering my generation had ever seen. Ethiopia would change my life forever.

CHAPTER THREE

WE ARE THE WORLD

*I was hungry and you gave me something to eat, I was thirsty and you
gave me something to drink,... I needed clothes and you clothed me, I was
sick and you looked after me... Matthew 25:35,36*

The field of grain had withered. The cattle were all dead.
The three-year drought and civil war had destroyed the crops of
the young, Ethiopian farmer, and now he and his family were
starving. His wife and three children were growing weaker every
day. One morning, he awoke and found that his son had died
during the night from hunger. He became frantic and terrified.

The farmer knew he could no longer remain on his own
land. He had heard about a place where he could get food for his
family, but it would take days of walking to reach it. He was
heartbroken over the loss of his child and could not bear the
thought of losing another, so he gathered his family and a few
items, and began the long journey.

Within one day, the farmer's family became too weak from
lack of food, to continue. He refused to allow them to die along
the road. Instead, he picked up his two small children and carried them for a mile and set them down to return for his wife. He
then picked her up and carried her the mile. He continued
repeating this mile by mile journey for three days until he stumbled into the feeding and health center where one of our medical
teams was working.

The will to survive is an extremely strong, innate desire.
However, the will to save another is an example of a great love.
The determination of the young farmer was not in vain. His family was saved. This would become one of many stories we brought
home from Ethiopia.

The preparations for our arrival in Ethiopia proved to be another interesting story. Getting our medical teams and supplies into Ethiopia was not a simple undertaking. One of our first obstacles was obtaining medical supplies. We began calling medical suppliers and hospitals asking for donations. Individuals were eager to help. It was not long before we had procured promises for those precious commodities from all over the country.

Our next assignments were more difficult. Tons of supplies needed to be gathered from all the different locations to one central place, and then transported to Ethiopia. To ship it all by boat would mean losing the ability of using the supplies for several months, which was out of the question. It was possible to send it by air freight, but the cost for shipping that many supplies was $300,000 to $400,000. We did not have that kind of money. We had procured over $500,000 worth of life-saving supplies and we had to get it there soon. We began to pray for a miracle.

The answer came from all the way across the country. One day, my phone rang. I answered, "Hello?"

"Hi," said the voice on the other end. "My name is Buddy Suggs with Eastern Airlines in Miami, Florida."

"How can I help you?" I asked.

He chuckled and responded, "I am calling to see if we could help you."

"I'm listening," I said.

"I heard you are going to send a medical team to Ethiopia. The employees of Eastern Airlines have seen the plight of the Ethiopians, and we wanted to do something as a group."

I found the words just slipping out of my mouth: "Can you get us an airplane to fly to Ethiopia with our supplies and our team?"

Buddy paused and then said, "Let me see what I can do. I'll call you back."

My heart skipped a few beats as I thought, "Lord is this you? Are you making this possible?"

The next day, Buddy called me back to let me know he had met with the corporate officers of Eastern. They had agreed to donate the use of one of their giant L-1011's if the employees could pay the $250,000 for fuel to get the plane there and back, and if they could secure a full flight crew to donate their own time.

I exclaimed, "Wow! Buddy, do you think it's possible to accomplish that?"

"It'll be tight," he answered, "but we'll approach everyone here to donate funds, and we'll mount a fundraising effort in the Miami area. Ron, could you come back here and we'll get you on radio and television stations to get the word out?"

"I'd be happy to do that," I said.

Soon, I was flying to Miami, scheduled to speak on many radio and television stations. Days later, Buddy told me they had the money needed, and a full crew willing to fly us. I could not believe all this had happened so quickly. Watching God work is an amazing experience.

When I told Buddy the supplies were stored at different locations, he answered, "Eastern flies all over the country. We'll pick it up at the various places and fly all of it to Miami to be put on the plane to Ethiopia."

I took a moment to thank God for the employees and corporate staff of Eastern Airlines. The efforts they had made to help the mission were unbelievable. Later, I learned they had worked so hard in raising funds for fueling the airplane that they had enough for a second flight. Thus, Eastern Corporate staff donated a second L-1011 to fly a second team and another $500,000 in medical supplies for the effort. The combined efforts of this group brought much-needed relief to dying people. Though Eastern is no longer in business, I will never forget the efforts of those wonderful people. I pray they will never forget the great thing they did that resulted in thousands of lives being saved.

Eastern Airlines picked up our first team in Seattle and returned us to Miami for our connecting flight. We had some technical difficulties and had to stay in Miami for a number of days before departing for Ethiopia. Being from the rainy Northwest, I thought a few extra days in Miami would be welcome. However, my biggest problem was keeping the team happy. They were anxious to arrive in Ethiopia where they were needed.

The day finally came when the big plane was loaded and ready. The excitement was easily discerned from the faces of the team members. My nerves were on edge. Some of those same questions I had back in 1979 returned to my thoughts. Would the team be able to perform what tasks were needed? What would it be like walking into a camp filled with 150,000 starving and sick people? Could we take care of all who were sick? When I finally boarded the plane, the weariness and relief from the stresses of getting the team off finally hit me, and I sat down and wept for joy.

A few minutes later, one of the pilots came to me and asked if I would like to sit in the cockpit. I was in the Air Force back in the 50s and flew in some big planes but I had never sat in the cockpit of something this big. It would be exciting.

When I entered the cockpit, I learned that I was in for more excitement than I thought. I overheard the pilot mention that we were within 1000 pounds of the airplane's limit. The Miami heat would also affect our takeoff. We were going to need a lot of runway. We taxied to the very end of the runway and the pilot revved up the engine. My heart beat faster. The pilot released the brake, and we started down the runway.

My anxiety was not lessened when the pilot began speaking to the airplane, "Come on baby, you can do it! Come on baby, let's get with it. I know you can, I know you can."

As he kept encouraging his gigantic steed, I looked ahead and saw the end of the runway. We still had not lifted. I began to silently plead, "Lord, I think we need some help here."

I could then see the fence at the end, and we were still not off the ground. I imagined our colossal jet crashing through the fence and tumbling over in a ball of fire, and then I heard the pilot say, "That's it, baby!"

I let out a long sigh, unaware that I had been holding my breath. The plane started lifting and slowly we were climbing upward. We probably cleared the fence by 300 feet, but from my vantage point it looked as if the bottom of the plane barely skimmed it.

During the trip, the volunteer flight crew of Eastern treated our team like royalty. It seemed we were all first class to them.

They did many extra services for our comfort. However, the highlight of the trip for the team was our approach into Addis Ababa airport.

In the distance, I could see the runway stretch out for miles and the feeling of "we made it" came over me. At the same moment, one of the flight crew put a song on over the intercom. The song had recently been recorded by many well-known musical artists to raise money for the Ethiopian famine, and it was titled, "We Are The World."

All of us wept. The song put into words what we were all feeling. We were all part of this human race. We belonged to each other, and we were responsible for each other. A fresh determination to help as many people as we could swept over our hearts.

It seemed as if the whole world was landing with us. The people of the world had reconciled their differences and come together as one to reach out to fellow citizens of the globe. I thought about all the volunteers: those who contributed money, the people who gave their time and services at the office, those involved with Eastern Airlines, and the many who bathed our team in prayer. Our carrying all this precious cargo would never have happened if hundreds of people had not gotten out of their chairs and done something to help. That young farmer, and many others, would be needing what we could give, and because of the many helping hands, we would give much. It was a vast and mighty team effort, and it echoed the vastness and mightiness of the God who was the beginning and the end of the entire project.

Give them Today
Therefore do not worry about tomorrow... Matthew 6:34

Once we arrived, we discovered that our large volunteer medical team would be split up and sent to a number of intensive feeding and health centers around the country of Ethiopia. This was a difficult adjustment, but I knew I would be visiting each group during my stay.

The first camp I flew into was located at an elevation of 8,000 feet. At night, the temperature dropped to nearly freezing.

The people there were ill-prepared for the cold. One young mother removed her burlap dress and placed it over her baby to keep her from dying from the cold. It was a perfect example of a mother's love for her child, and I would see this again and again, wherever I visited a tragedy.

Nearly 100,000 ghostly figures waited around the feeding and health center, and the emaciated forms of the people made it look like a Nazi concentration camp from World War II. Many times one could not tell a woman from a man because their bodies were so shrunken.

At the health clinic where our own medical team was working, quick adaptations to the horrid conditions were being made. It only took the team a day to realize that the nurses would have to serve as doctors. There were so many who needed care and only a few doctors. Once they saw what most of the people suffered from, it became easy for the nurses to diagnose patients.

On the particular day when I visited our clinic, I saw two nurses attempt to get an IV started on a severely dehydrated baby. They could not reach a vein because the veins had collapsed. They gave a desperate effort. Later that day, I asked one of the nurses, Marie Davis, if they had been successful. Tears welled up in her eyes as she said, "We lost the baby. It's awful. Every night, I go back to my tent and get on my knees, asking God to forgive me for not saving more."

My heart ached for her, yet it also beat with pride for the nobility of our team. These wonderful volunteers were working every minute they could, saving hundreds, yet they mourned every per-

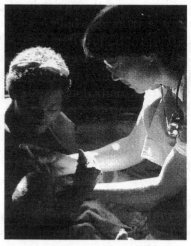

Nurse Kathy Solmonson treats a baby with Cholera in Ethiopia. Photo courtesy of Michael Lloyd, *The Oregonian*

son that was lost. They truly recognized the worth of each life. I put my arms around this compassionate woman and reminded her that she could not hold herself responsible for every life. That was God's job. God was pleased with what good she had done. He was pleased that she had decided to labor for His harvest.

In the midst of tragedy, humor was needed. Each day, the team ritual was to roll out of their sleeping bags and begin the contest to see who had the most new flea bites on their bodies. Marie laughed as she told me she counted over 250 bites on herself. Though there was very little physical comfort, the humor helped to encourage us. It was both physically and emotionally exhausting work.

One of our nurses, Diane Van Order, was interviewed by a television news team and the reporter asked, "Diane, what do you think you can accomplish among all these sick and dying people?"

Diane thought for a moment and said, "Well, I guess we are giving them today. Maybe they will have tomorrow."

Diane spoke the words that would become our motto for the mission. It would go on our printing and would be placed on the walls of our offices, to remind us of our focus. On my office, there hangs a decorous plaque that says, "We give them today, so they may have tomorrow."

Photo courtesy of Marie Davis in Ethiopia.

People have since asked me similar questions. "What does it matter?" "What can one do amongst so many?" "Does the work mean anything when there would be another famine or war within a few years that would kill them?"

In my heart I whisper my response, so what? If another catastrophe hits those we have helped, they still had a few more days to experience the good gifts God has given us, to love their families, and be loved. Aren't we all doing the same thing? Prolonging our days against that inevitable time?

It is hard to answer such questions, for they do not mean anything until one has helped others in such terrible circumstances. When I look into the faces of a young mother and father who had four children, but now only one remains, it is easy to see the importance of that one life. The parents desperately want to see their child survive. They have hopes, just like our own, of watching that child grow into an adult to have children of his own.

Our needs and desires cross all political and cultural boundaries. We all love our children and want the best for them.

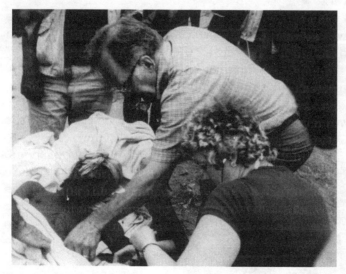

Dr. Travis Cavens and Nurse Diane Van Order helping a cholera patient during the 1984 famine in Ethiopia. Photo courtesy of Michael Lloyd, *The Oregonian*

When we begin guessing the futures of people, and in response don't help them, we are playing God. We cannot see into the future as God can. A today could become years of tomorrows. Refusing help is almost certain death.

The young Ethiopian father who endured such pain to carry his family to our clinic was very thankful for our team giving his family "today." I believe that the children of that young father are alive today with families of their own. So, when people ask whether what we do really matters, my answer is "God only knows," and then I add, "However, when I see the joy on the faces of parents when our team gives their child another chance, it matters to me."

Life or Death Decisions

Are not five sparrows sold for two pennies? Yet not one of them is forgotten by God. Luke 12:6

One day, I watched a young doctor on our team, Dr. Jay Kravitz, as he examined two young boys who were very ill. The boys were lifeless. They could not even raise their heads up from the bed.

I looked at the boys' father and could not help wondering how I would feel if these were my children. Tears welled up in my eyes as I sensed the father's fear. His eyes showed his emotions: sad and afraid.

Dr. Kravitz had trouble diagnosing their illness. Since we did not have the testing equipment as we did in the States, he could only treat them for what he thought they might have. If he was right, maybe they would live. If he was wrong, they would be dead in the morning. He looked at the boys intently, his brow furrowed in thought. Finally, he made a decision. As he mixed up the ingredients for the medication, he said to a nurse, "I'm not sure they will make it. We will see in the morning."

For most of these medical professionals, it was uncommon for them to make life or death decisions at home. When those decisions came up, they had all the medical technology needed at their fingertips, as well as a knowledgeable staff on which to rely. But we were not in America, and in Ethiopia, life or death decisions were part of the daily routine. Yet, the fact that it was routine did not seem to make the decisions any easier.

Non-medical people probably have a difficult time imagining the stress and pressure of such a decision. Before you, lies a patient. The symptoms are confusing. The possibilities of the diagnosis are many. The patient is dying. For a moment, this life lying on the bed before you is in your hands. The responsibility and burden of this choice must be immense.

That night, those two boys were in my thoughts. I prayed the Lord would use Dr. Kravitz's diagnosis and allow the boys to live. The next morning the team went to the tent where the boys were staying. To our amazement, they were sitting up and taking food! The young father was beaming as he watched his sons eat.

Dr. Kravitz' smile was one of huge relief. He had guessed right! The burden of these two boys' lives were lifted from his shoulders. He had done his part to give them today, so they might have tomorrow.

There were other life or death decisions that did not turn out so well. I flew to another camp where there were over 150,000 hungry people. Each morning, 1,400 mothers with their starving babies would line up in neat lines. Each mother hoped her baby would be admitted to the intensive feeding program held behind the gate. Only 200 of the worst cases could be admitted each day, due to the limitations on room and food. The tragedy was that all the babies seemed like worst cases.

Every morning, our nurses would go down the line of mothers and would feel between the fingers of the babies, trying to determine their fat content. The nurses knew that some of the babies they did not select would most likely die by the next day. In other words, they were virtually choosing who would live and who would die.

Often I have wished I were a medical person so I could help, but not at these moments. These brave nurses would complete their selection, and then rush to a quiet place and sob out their heartache. The burdens they were carrying were so heavy, and they each did it willingly. Yet, choosing to be there did not make it easier.

Empty Buckets
Freely you have received, freely give. Matthew 10:8

One of those mornings, as I watched the nurses walking down the long line of starving women and babies, I spotted two elderly women in the distance walking straight towards me. Each had a small plastic bucket in her hands, in hopes of finding grain.

45

They stopped just a few feet in front of me. Within a few seconds, one of the ladies started to tremble violently and fell to the ground. Nurses rushed to her aid, but it was too late. She died that morning, just a few feet from help.

Later, a photographer took a picture of her, and gave it to me. She was an elderly woman, and when she died she was lying on her side. Her arm was outstretched and inches from her hand lay the bucket which had carried her hopes of finding grain, and had dropped from her hand, empty. I have the photograph in my office, but I do not need it. The image of that dead woman was etched into my memory forever. God will never let me forget her.

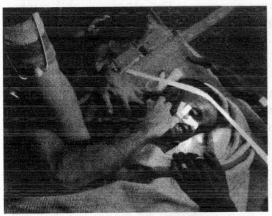

Dr. Jay Kravitz attempts to save a child in 1984 during the famine in Ethiopia. Michael Lloyd, *The Oregonian*

The bucket is a symbol to me. Whenever my commitment to this mission wanes, I see millions of empty buckets representing needs: hunger, sickness, shelter, ...and loneliness.

When I returned home from Ethiopia, I would wake in the middle of the night and cry as I relived some of those scenes. I began to understand what some of the Viet Nam veterans felt as they relived their experiences in the war. Ethiopia changed my perception of my own country. I was more open to the needs in America. Nothing was the same for me. Everywhere I looked, I saw needy people.

A burning desire to communicate what I had witnessed welled up inside me. It was my job to speak for the millions of suffering people around the world. The difficulty of sharing the many needs with those who haven't experienced anything like what I had was great. My friends told me to just share the truth from my heart, which I tried to do.

To communicate what was in my heart, I had to draw a picture in people's minds of the lady with the empty bucket. God gave me that memory, so I would always remember the empty buckets in our world. He also gave that memory to me so I would share it with others. Americans have been so blessed. God intended for us to share with those who have nothing. We need to take from our bucket to fill someone else's. When people take this step, a wonderful thing happens. The other person's bucket begins to fill, but ours never goes dry.

* * * * *

My experiences in Ethiopia would serve as a base for my desire to help hurting people for the rest of my life. After Ethiopia, there was no question about whether Northwest Medical teams

Ethiopian woman who came searching for food during the Ethiopian famine of 1984. She died before Ron Post with an empty bucket in her hand. Photo courtesy of NWMT.

would be a permanent mission. For the next several years, we were going to be involved with many more famines and disasters.

CHAPTER FOUR

EARTHQUAKE

*At this my heart pounds and leaps from its place. Listen! Listen to the roar
of his voice, to the rumbling that comes from his mouth. Job 37:1,2*

We loaded the team and supplies into a couple of taxis and
headed for the U. S. Embassy. It was a vast city, with its many
sky scrapers, colonial style buildings, and 20 million people.
Now, its sky scrapers had toppled, its colonial style buildings had
crumpled, and its 20 million people were either dead or in a panic.
We could not believe the destruction. We were later told that
5,900 major buildings were destroyed or heavily damaged. People
were milling about the streets, afraid to go back inside. Their confused and frightened expressions showed plainly on their faces,
and they walked around slowly, as if they were in a daze.

The taxi driver had to choose side streets to avoid the rubble. We had been driving for two hours; two days ago, it would
have taken us just a half hour to reach our destination. Several
times, the driver wanted to quit, but I urged him to continue.
Finally, within three blocks of the embassy, we were stalled in
heavy traffic.

It had been nearly three hours since we left the airport. The
driver was getting impatient, and said, "We cannot make it. We
must quit!" However, I would not let him quit. A way must be
found.

A shock of surprise went through me. At first, I thought
someone had started rocking the car. I turned around, but did
not see anyone. I could almost smell the fear in the air. I looked
up, and my heart began to race. The light poles that lined the
street were shaking back and forth violently, like gigantic fishing
poles with fighting fish on the other ends. One of the team mem-

bers screamed, "Earthquake!" The ground beneath us was heaving. People ran out of the buildings screaming. Some dropped to their knees to pray. They must have felt that the world was truly coming to an end, that the ground would open up and swallow them.

Then, everything was still in Mexico City.

Why?

Then a great and powerful wind tore the mountains apart and shattered the rocks before the Lord, but the Lord was not in the wind. After the wind there was an earthquake, but the Lord was not in the earthquake. After the earthquake came a fire, but the Lord was not in the fire. And after the fire came a gentle whisper. When Elijah heard it, ... he went out and stood at the mouth of the cave. I Kings 19:11-13

Ethiopia was a clear call. The needs were great, and it was easy to know we should go and help. However, other times, the call would not be so easily discerned. There would be many occasions when I would risk losing face for venturing into unknown territory.

Mexico City was just such an incident. In September, 1985, the world's largest city was shattered by a powerful earthquake, measured as an 8.4 on the Richter scale. All power, telephones, television, and radio had been cut, making it impossible to send out or receive communications. Therefore, the news was sketchy. Reporters guessed thousands were dead, thousands injured, and hundreds of thousands were homeless. Immediately, I wondered whether Northwest Medical Teams could help. However, the news stories contradicted each other. One report said that the airport was closed because of severe damage. Other reports said the airport was open. Some reports indicated that the Mexican government was requesting no help, yet others said thousands needed medical care. My mind raced as I tried to decide the path our team should take. Should we rush down there with a medical team? One friend said, "Ron, if you are not needed, won't it make you look bad?"

Following the example of biblical leaders when faced with a

problem, I retreated to be alone with God. I decided to ask the Lord to give me direction. The reports were too unclear. The advice from friends wasn't unified. I needed to make sure that the decision I made would be one I could stand by, even if it failed. As I sought God's direction, one thought kept returning to my mind, "Don't worry about what people may think. Do what is right."

I shared this with Jean and she gave me a confirmation. "Do what your heart is telling you, Ron," she said.

So I did. In the next few minutes, I was calling the country's national airline, Mexicana Airlines, and asking them if they would fly our team and supplies to Mexico City. They agreed. The next day, which was the day after the earthquake, we flew to Mexico City. The airport had opened again. Later, we learned from the U.S. Embassy that we were the first American team to arrive for the disaster.

In spite of the reluctant taxi driver and the second earthquake (an 8.2 on the Richter scale we found out later), we did arrive at the U.S. Embassy. There we met with Sandy Del Prado. Sandy worked in the U.S.A.I.D. (United States Agency for International Development) office. I introduced myself and the team, and told her we were from Oregon.

Sandy exclaimed, "I am, too!" We were instantly friends. Sandy gave us more details on the damage and the problems we would face. Sandy and her husband, Guido, who also worked for the state department, insisted we stay in their home where they fed and cared for our team.

The next day, Sandy introduced us to a representative of the Mexican Red Cross. When they discovered we were a medical team, they stuck us in the back of an ambulance and told the driver to take us to the collapsed buildings where people were being pulled from the rubble. The ride was frightening as the driver sped down wrong way streets against traffic with the red lights flashing.

We finally arrived at three twelve-story apartment buildings that had collapsed. In each of these buildings, 1000 tenants were renting. Now, thousands were dead. We got out of the ambulance, and stood by to help survivors as they were pulled out of the crumpled concrete and other debris. Hour after hour, we waited.

The work of the rescuers was difficult. Crawling over the rubble was life-threatening, yet they doggedly searched, hoping to find survivors. Often, noisy machinery would buzz in the background. Suddenly, someone would yell, "Quiet!" A total hush would fall over the place. Everyone listened carefully for a voice crying out from within the heap of concrete. It was a strange moment, experiencing the eerie quietude. Sadly, the hush was often in vain. They were not finding many survivors. Later, the U.S. Embassy estimated that approximately 30,000 to 40,000 people died.

When we realized we could do little to help, we tried another place. The Medical Training Hospital had been reduced to a pile of concrete. Six hundred doctors and nurses were buried. Again, we waited. On we went from place to place, looking at the destruction, but finding little to do. We were not helping, and we felt discouraged.

The next day, the Salvation Army set up a tent where many of the homeless were camping. Food and drinks were served. Many of the homeless needed treatment for cuts and minor sicknesses, so our team began to meet those needs. However, treating these minor injuries was not what I had expected, and disappointment pervaded the group.

The return from Mexico gave me very little satisfaction. The trip seemed to have been without a purpose. Had I misread my heart? Should I have waited longer for more information? A few team volunteers expressed that they had wasted their time. One doctor who had served in Ethiopia, and then in Mexico, was so discouraged that he never volunteered again. My heart was heavy. How could I have read it so wrong? I had felt so sure about going.

These doubts wrestled within me, and then I decided to give them to God. During my prayer time, I asked Him the question that He probably hears far too often: why? It would be nearly four long months before I would have an answer.

God's Plan

Commit to the Lord whatever you do, and your plans will succeed.
Proverbs 16:3

It was January, 1986, when I received a telephone call from Sandy Del Prado at the U.S. Embassy. "Ron, we need your team badly," she said. "The earthquake left nearly 500,000 people homeless. They are living on the streets, in parks, and parking lots. Some only have cardboard or blankets to make their housing. It has turned cold at night and thousands of children have developed serious problems. Many children have already died. Can you bring a medical team to help these people?"

Without much thought, I answered, yes.

A team of doctors and nurses were quickly assembled, and once again, Mexicana Airlines flew the team to Mexico City. Sandy met us at the airport and insisted we stay in their home. She showed us where many of the homeless were encamped. I began looking for a place to set up a clinic. Many of the buildings were damaged or weakened, so it was difficult. Finally, a warehouse building was found, but much of the roof had been damaged, leaving a huge hole. Inside, we set up a couple of tents and opened the clinic. Within an hour, we had a line of sick people two blocks long waiting to get help.

Jean had accompanied me on this trip. Though she is not medically trained, she found ways to be helpful by taking babies who were burning up with fever and swabbing them with cold water. I was very proud of the way she helped. Every person on the team worked hard trying to examine as many sick people as possible. At night, they fell into their beds, completely exhausted.

Some Mexican friends showed me the city, which awakened me to the overwhelming poverty. Three-thousand people were moving into the city each day from the various states. Work was unavailable where they lived and they came searching for employment. However, there were no jobs. My friends shared more staggering statistics: six million people in the city were unemployed, and another six million were earning less than a dollar a day.

Many had started squatter communities on the hillsides around Mexico City, because there was nowhere to live. They made houses of cardboard, scrap tin or boards they found. They were hungry and lacked medical care.

The mass poverty I saw was unbelievable. Seeing the poverty of Mexico City launched Northwest Medical Teams into an outreach that continues in Mexico today. Thousands of lives have been changed.

Mixed Signals

Call to Me, and I will answer by revealing what is hard and hidden, what you do not know! Jeremiah 33:3

A disastrous earthquake struck San Salvador, El Salvador in 1986. Once again, all communication in and out of the country had been disrupted. The same questions that I faced with the Mexico disaster rose up before me once again. Should we go? If so, what kind of medical response would be needed?

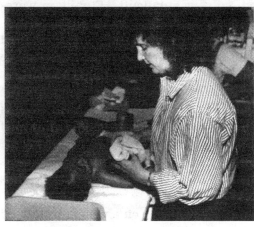

Jean Post sponging a child with a high fever at a makeshift clinic after an earthquake struck Mexico City in 1985. Over 500,000 people were left homeless on the streets. Photo, NWMT.

There were no reports on the situation, except for one from the United States State Department. I called them, and asked if they knew about the conditions. A representative said, "You are not needed. The El Salvador government will turn any aid mission around if you decide to land."

With a report like that, I decided to wait. Then, I received a phone call from my friend, Buddy Suggs, of Eastern Airlines in Miami. "We intercepted a ham radio call from a Salvadoran doctor pleading for help," Buddy said. "He said that many people have suffered from broken bones."

How I would have loved to talk with this Salvadoran doctor! I called the state department again, and they repeated, "Do not go. You will be turned away."

I was confused by these mixed signals. It seemed like we should be able to trust our state department, but the plea of that doctor could not be pushed away. I prayed for direction, and when I was finished, I decided we would take an orthopedic team. I did not know a thing about orthopedics. I had never been to an orthopedic doctor in my life. This was definitely new territory.

A valuable lesson I learned from running this mission is this: when you don't know, find out who does. I called a doctor friend and asked him if he knew an orthopedic doctor I could contact. He could not have guided me to a better person. Dr. Jerry Becker in Salem, Oregon, turned out to be a tremendous help for the Salvadoran situation, as well as many future missions. The information about the team and the proper tools and orthopedic supplies we would need was soon jotted down on the paper in front of me.

Bravely, I decided to ask him for one more small favor, "Would you come with us?"

Without hesitation, he answered, "Yes."

Jean began arranging air travel, while I assembled a medical team. Later, I called the Office of Foreign Disaster at the U.S. State Department to tell them we were going. They said, "We cannot stop you, but we do not recommend it."

With much prayer, we departed. A lot of apprehension was in my heart when we landed at the San Salvador airport. What if they did turn us back? Would the medical team be embarrassed? Would they ever trust me again? We walked off the plane into the waiting area. Immediately, a man walked purposefully toward me, and asked, "Are you Ron Post?"

"Yes," I replied, wondering whether we were in trouble.

He smiled, and said, "Hello. I work with the U.S. Office of Foreign Disaster Team." He shook the team members' hands, and then added, "The U.S. State Department radioed us about your arrival. There are vans outside to take your team to a hospital where you can work. We are so glad you are here." I could not believe my ears!

I whispered, "Thank you Lord." Then, we walked out to where the vans were parked.

As we were driving to the hospital, we were given more details about the situation. The earthquake was only measured a five at the epicenter, which would usually not cause much damage. However, the earthquake occurred directly under the city. Because most of the buildings were made of adobe and bamboo, they came crashing down on the people.

As we approached the city, the vast destruction became evident. It looked as if a gigantic monster had had a tantrum and had stomped all over his model city. Hundreds of buildings were reduced to a pile of rubble. Several large hotels were tilting over as though they could fall any time. Most of the main hospitals had been severely damaged and were closed, making it more difficult for people to get help.

Other factors compounded the terrible conditions. There was also a civil war. Everywhere we went, the streets were full of armed soldiers. Some of them looked like children, holding guns which were almost taller than them. We were told the soldiers were very edgy. A truckload of people crossed an intersection just the day before our arrival. Someone dropped a bottle from the truck, making a popping noise. The young soldiers fired on the truck, killing one person. Also, several Americans had been shot in the restaurant of a major hotel. We were told to be very careful where we went.

We arrived at one of the main hospitals in the city and unloaded our boxes. The hospital administrator welcomed us and introduced us to the doctor in charge of orthopedics. Though I could not speak Spanish, it was easy to observe that the doctor was not pleased we were there. First, he told us he only had one orthopedic surgery room available and he was using it. In response, one of our team members suggested we could take almost any room and turn it into an operating room.

The doctor reluctantly agreed, and guided us to a storage room. However, he offered no help. Unaffected by his manner, our team quickly started converting the room. They carried boxes out of the storeroom and sanitized the room. While they were busy, I tried to discover how we might have offended the orthopedic doctor.

A meeting with the doctor and the administrator quickly answered my questions. The professional's ego was wounded. Though he could not take care of all the cases, his pride would be offended to let American doctors help. The administrator simply shrugged his shoulders as though to say, "What can I do?"

When I told the team the news, a silence followed. They were obviously disappointed. We sat there, stumped, as to what to do next. The idea of returning home was unthinkable, when we knew help was needed. Yet, other options were vague.

I was still sitting in that storage room, thinking, when a volunteer nurse, Marie Davis, approached me. "Ron, you have to hear what this young Salvadoran doctor has to say," she said, excitedly.

In excellent English, the man introduced himself and explained his reasons for approaching us. "Hello," he said with a warm smile. "My name is Dr. Jose Palomo. I am an intern who has been temporarily assigned to this hospital. My regular assignment is with the hospital in Santa Anna, which is an hour or so from San Salvador." His countenance became somber. He explained, "There are many patients with fractured bones and no one is available to repair them. They have been lying in beds for 13 days now." He shook his head sadly, and added, "Some people are suffering from fractured hips and broken limbs that protrude through the skin. They have not been attended to because of the number of disaster victims." He looked straight into my eyes. "Please, come and help us!"

Of course, we went without hesitation. After acquiring transportation, we loaded the supplies and drove away. After dark, we pulled up to the hospital. Our doctors made some quick rounds, and confirmed what Dr. Palomo had said. People were suffering with open fractured legs, broken pelvises and other major breaks that the medical staff at the hospital had been unable to handle.

Other problems were discovered as well. Proper orthopedic supplies were scarce. There were very few of the special pins and screws needed to repair badly broken bones. The X-ray machine was in poor condition, and there was no qualified technician to read the X-rays. They were also short on antibiotics to fight infection, and pain medication. These patients had lain there for days, taking only aspirin for relief of pain.

Dr. Becker had planned well in choosing which orthopedic supplies to bring, but the need was more than he predicted. Once more, the team met to plan. They prepared a list. Antibiotics, which were very expensive, was the first item. A portable X-ray machine was next. The acting secretary busily scribbled item after item. Then, Dr. Becker instructed me to contact an orthopedic technician in Salem, named Jim Bowlin. "If anyone can get these necessary items together, it's Jim," said Dr. Becker. "See if you can get him to come, too," he added. I understood his plan: though we already had one orthopedic technician, Harry Martin, we could do much more by having two operating teams.

Rushing to a telephone, I prayed that the system would be working again. The phone rang, and Jean answered. It was just shy of 5 p.m., and she was still at the office. Not knowing how long the call would hold, I just told her the facts, needs, and the name Jim Bowlin. She understood the importance of getting the items donated. We did not have the funds to purchase airline tickets or freight.

Jean would prove her worth as a trooper in the mission. She called the airline of El Salvador, Taca Airlines, and explained what we were trying to accomplish. They offered to fly, not only a passenger (the technician), but all the boxes of supplies.

Going to a disaster in El Salvador was the last thing Jim Bowlin had on his mind when Jean contacted him. He had two tickets in his hand that meant a great deal to him: special seats to the world series game. He loved baseball, and finally his favorite team would be playing in the big one.

Rather than assuming that Jean would find another technician, Jim gave up his tickets. To some, this choice did not make sense. However, Jim had a priority list in his heart that placed others above self.

After he had completed his work in El Salvador, I asked him, "Was the decision to go difficult?"

Jim responded, "I am a trained medical person. Helping people is why I went into medicine. When the request came from Dr. Becker, I could not turn my back on it."

I followed with another question, "Was going to El Salvador worth it?"

Jim answered, "Going to El Salvador opened my eyes to see how very fortunate I am to live and work in America." He added, "We have so much, and they have so little. If people here could go to a place like that just once and see the needs, they would not find it hard to give up something they felt was important."

Once Jim arrived with the supplies, our team quickly triaged the patients to make sure they worked on the worst cases first. Then, they worked day and night performing one surgery after another. However, even though we had a second orthopedic doctor, Dr. Bertram Robertson, we could not accommodate the number of surgeries needed to be done. Every day these patients went without corrective surgery, the harder it would be to repair the damage. We needed help.

Help would come from the Salvation Army. They had set up a tent in downtown San Salvador to provide care to the homeless from the earthquake. It was discovered that two orthopedic surgeons from California were working in the tent. One of our team members contacted these doctors and found the Salvation Army really needed nurses at that time. We had nurses on our team. So, we traded. Marie Davis and Shari Pfeiffer worked in the Salvation Army tent, and the two orthopedic surgeons joined our surgery team. Some would say, "What a coincidence!" I know better than to believe that. A more apt saying would be, "God works in mysterious ways."

Dr. Becker organized the surgery team into smaller teams and gave them surgery schedules. Soon, all the victims had been cared for.

There were other wonderful results that came of our going to El Salvador. Dr. Palomo, the young Salvadoran doctor who had asked us to come help his people, worked alongside our doctors. He was so enthralled by what he saw, he decided he wanted to become an orthopedic surgeon. Later, he left for France to study orthopedic medicine. Afterwards, Dr. Ken Pierce, a neurosurgeon on our team, was able to get Dr. Palomo an intern position at his hospital in Seattle, Washington, to study for six months. Today, Dr. Palomo is considered the best orthopedic surgeon in El Salvador.

Another Salvadoran man had been shaken out of a tree by the earthquake and was paralyzed with a back injury. Dr. Pierce examined Daniel Lopez Valencia and said, "We could help you walk again, if we could straighten your spine and hold it in place with Steffee screws and plates." Unfortunately, there were none of this kind of screws and plates available in the country.

When we returned to the states, Dr. Pierce received approval from the Group Health Hospital in Seattle to allow this man to come there for surgery. We arranged travel for him. Dr. Jerry Becker, who had stayed on in El Salvador after the team had returned to the United States, agreed to accompany Daniel to Seattle. He wrapped him in a plaster cast to prevent injury to his spine and took care of him all the way home.

Dr. Pierce performed the surgery. It was an exciting day when we saw this man walk again. Today he is still walking with the aid of a cane. Without the help of our team, he would never have had a chance to walk again.

Listen to your Heart
Wisdom reposes in the heart of the discerning... Proverbs 14:33

The lesson I learned in dealing with the Mexico and El Salvador earthquakes was to trust my heart. God speaks to us through our hearts, which is the core of our being. When our hearts are in God's control, they are trustworthy. God showed me that by abiding in Him, I can discover the course He wants me to follow, and God's ways will always succeed. Success does not always happen the way we expect, yet there is a victory to be found in any endeavor. God will eventually reveal the answer to the "why" we ask Him.

Risking money and time in an outreach is rarely unwise. Someone once said, "When you wish you could help someone, but don't, it's only wishful thinking. When you dream of doing something noble but don't, it's only a noble dream." Some causes are so worthy, that even failing at them is noble. I believe Northwest Medical Teams serves such a cause.

Fearing failure keeps many people in their easy chairs, rather than reaching out to others. A perfectionist could never succeed at the tasks in which our group had been involved. None of our missions were performed with perfection, yet we had accomplished more things than we could ever have imagined possible, simply because we tried. God promises that "I can do everything through Him who gives me strength" (Philippians 4:13).

What if we had not gone to Mexico? Had we not gone, we would not have seen the poverty and needs of our neighbor. Seeing it has resulted in health clinics, feeding programs, agriculture training, water and sanitation systems, and thousands helped through our surgery program. We cannot count the lives that have been touched and changed as a result of God using our efforts.

We also have been blessed immensely. We have a deep joy that comes only by serving others. We have made wonderful friends, helped them in their suffering and shared the person of Jesus Christ with untold thousands.

If we had not risked failure in El Salvador, many people would still be suffering. Daniel Valencia would never have walked again. Dr. Jose Palomo would never have found his calling. In turn, Dr. Palomo's practice has helped hundreds of his people.

It only takes one person to get up from his or her easy chair to begin a chain of people getting up from theirs. We will never fully know all the lives that have been touched over the years. Only God knows the full extent. Yet, we do not need to be concerned with numbers and results. Our calling is simple: take care of the sick, the hungry, and the hurting, even if it is risky.

To laugh is to risk appearing the fool. To weep is to risk appearing sentimental. To reach out for another is to risk involvement. To expose feelings is to risk exposing your true self. To place your ideas, your dreams, before a crowd is to risk their loss. To love is to risk not being loved in return. To live is to risk dying. To hope is to risk despair. To try is to risk failure. But risks must be taken, because the greatest hazard in life is to risk nothing. The person who risks nothing, does nothing, has nothing, and is nothing. They may avoid suffering and sorrow, but they cannot learn, feel, change, grow, love, live. Only a person who risks is free.

Anonymous

CHAPTER FIVE

GOD'S PEOPLE

Speak, LORD, for your servant is listening. 1 *Samuel 3:9*

A gorgeous summer day had emerged. The sun had chased all the clouds away and shone with its characteristic lone brilliance that is unequaled. A childhood experience came back to me in a flash of memory. I was running across our acreage in California, barefoot. The wind seemed to give me a push from behind, and I felt that I was running so fast, I might take off at any moment.

We stepped out of the van, and my childhood memory seemed to slap me in the face. Rather than a fresh breeze wafting easily by, the smell of rotten garbage sat still and stale around us. It filled our nostrils and sent our stomachs into spasms. When the wind did come, it whipped gritty dust into my face and eyes.

Here, children ran barefoot through the brilliant morning; yet, they ran over broken glass, metal, and rotten food, not meadow grass. Filthy and tattered clothing covered the neglected small bodies. The children's hair was so matted, it looked as though someone had poured glue on their heads. Grime covered their faces, and green mucous seeped from their noses, indicating infection to even the non-medical people.

Rather than a mountain of soil and rock, towering heaps of junk, discarded scraps, and other wastes were these people's mountain view. Like mountain villages nestled into the little valleys, groups of shacks pressed into cracks and crevices of the mounds of *basura*, or garbage. The materials for the shacks were collected from the heap they lived on — cardboard, tarpaper, or anything else they could find. The flooring was dirt spread over the filth. A pack of mangy, disease-riddled dogs ran by. Pigs rooted through the garbage. The squalor was sickening.

Fifty-gallon barrels lined the front of the shacks. Dead flies floated on the surface of the water that filled them. I asked one of the occupants through an interpreter, "How do you use this water?"

The answer was as I had feared. "This is our drinking and cooking water," he said. "The water is trucked into the dump and pumped into the barrels." Later, I would learn that the water they pumped in was contaminated. Moreover, the barrels had contained chemicals previously, and the people did not boil their water before drinking it.

I approached one shack and Lalo, my Mexican volunteer, introduced me to another occupant. I learned that the woman was in her forties, but she looked much older. Since she was a child, her life had been spent working in the dump every day. "I am the third generation of my family to live in this place," she said. "My name is Carmen. I also have raised my son here, and now I am raising my grandson, Auturo." Carmen ladled some hot, watery beans into a bowl for her son and Auturo. Within a few seconds, flies floated on the surface of the bowl of beans. The flies were everywhere, and they constantly swarmed our heads.

I looked at Auturo and wondered about his future. "Is this the only life he can have?" I asked myself. "Is there more than this?" Within a few years after I met Carmen, she died. It was a life cut short by her environment. She had never left the dump in which she had been raised.

Carmen was among the hundreds of "trash pickers" who lived on the Las Aguilas Dump in the north part of Mexico City. These people picked through the piles of refuse that were dumped daily from trucks, searching for recyclable materials to sell or to use for food to eat. This was their daily routine from their childhood until they were so old and stooped they could not walk anymore. Then, they would hope a son or daughter would feed them until they died. This was their existence.

Jean and I went back to our hotel room and wept. Our hearts were broken. "These are your people, Lord. People who you have hand-crafted are living in a garbage dump with little food and shelter." God's heart was as broken as mine, I knew. He must have been weeping as he guided me to that scene. A story came into my mind as I prayed.

In the midst of a tragedy, a man yelled out, "Where is God in all of this?"

A voice answered him, saying, "Where are my people?"

I imagined God asking this question of me, and I answered as Samuel did when God called him, "Here I am; you called me."

Jean and I decided in that hotel room that we would do all we could to reach out to the "trash-pickers".

Medical clinics were needed for the people of the dump, as well as the many earthquake victims left in homeless squatter communities springing up all around Mexico City. This would be a big step for the mission. Before, our outreach was always temporary. We went, did our work, and we left. The outreach to Mexico City would be long-term. Would our board want to make this kind of commitment?

Jean and I decided to return home with the purpose of approaching the board with the request. I shared the needs of the people I saw, and we discussed how this commitment would be different from past outreaches. Our board has always had members who are compassionate and have a deep love for God. I finished sharing my report, and tears filled many eyes. When we adjourned, the consensus was that we should do everything possible to improve the lives of these people.

To accomplish our goals in Mexico, we would need more money. At the time of our consensus, the mission was weathering a financial crisis. Our donation level in 1986 was only about $4,000 a month, which was not enough to support our dreams for Mexico.

There were many decisions the Lord helped me to make in founding the mission. The first was that I would not be the owner. The mission would belong to the Lord. Anyone else involved would have his or her own responsibilities for carrying out the mission's goals. This decision helped to separate the mission from my business experiences before. Businesses I had previously owned over the years were ones I produced until they were successful. I would then sell making a profit from my hard work. However, the purpose of this mission was to involve as many people as I could in God's plans. It was an opportunity for those who wanted to participate in something meaningful. If the mission succeeded, God deserved the glory and not me.

Secondly, I decided that we would always pay our debts. As a Christian, if I owe a debt to someone, I must find a way to pay it. How could I possibly be Jesus' servant while breaking my word? This issue was so important to me that I vowed I would shut the mission down if ever the time came when we could not pay our bills.

As a part of my report to the board, I shared the advice given me by a fundraising consultant. He recommended we hold fundraising banquets. Naturally, the board had its concerns. How many would attend? Would the banquets contribute enough for significant finances to pay the needs we had? Who would organize the banquets? After a time of prayer, the board decided we should try the advice. We began asking a few friends if they would fill banquet tables with friends, family and associates.

Soon, the first banquet commenced. The format for the evening was simple: volunteers would describe their experiences while serving in the field. There were some emotional stories told. As for myself, I felt very nervous about what I would say and just how effectively I could challenge those who attended to participate financially. A friend advised me to simply share what God had placed in my heart. I still abide by that advice now.

Plainly, I asked people to give. It was easier than I thought, because I was not asking for myself, but for those we served. Being forthright and direct gave me the confidence to share my heart's desires, and the people listened. Our first banquet was a smashing success. The 400 people in attendance responded by pledging over $40,000! Truly, God had answered the questions asked by the board. We felt secure at that time to make the commitment to Mexico.

Fund-raising banquets became a major tool used to support the work of NWMT. The banquets also served to update donors on the latest work programs and to celebrate together what had been accomplished.

We wanted to hold banquets all over the Northwest, but this part of the ministry needed a person to oversee its success. The job required a hard-worker who could enlist the help of volunteers from the different regions. My wife, Jean, stepped into this difficult and challenging role, and has lead and developed our banquets all over the Northwest. At the height of our banquet years, we were holding 21 per year. Previous team members readily volunteered because Jean had such a passion for what she was doing. Though exhausting at times, the job also was a joyful blessing for Jean. It is wonderful to watch how God has a special place for each of us in His work.

We were also waiting for God to fill another special role — the director of the work in Mexico. It was important that the mission in Mexico would not be run by the "big North American brother." Mexican Nationals had to be at the heart of it. We would provide the funding, and many American volunteers would help. However, we searched for a Mexican director who was trustworthy and who would be committed to the task.

Jean and I traveled back to Mexico City and shared this concern with the young Mexican volunteer, Lalo Martinez, who had guided us before. Later that evening, Lalo called me and said, "There is a man who attends my church who I believe would be an excellent director. He has been involved in business, and now is managing commercial properties." Lalo paused, and asked, "Would you like to meet him?"

"Yes," was my reply. "Could Jean and I meet with him for breakfast tomorrow?"

The next morning we were introduced to a man named Antonio Vazquez. We began talking about the needs, and what we visualized developing. Within minutes, Jean and I came to the same conclusion. We both sensed this was someone very special at our table. Within a lifetime, there are few people of this caliber one might meet. Everything within us said, "This is the person God wants to lead this work."

We asked Antonio that morning if he would take the job of

running the work in Mexico. Wisely, he asked for time to pray and discuss it with his family. The next morning, Antonio accepted the job. I have never been more sure of a person. This dear, compassionate, Jesus-loving, hardworking man would become one of my best friends. He would develop a staff of committed Christians and begin new programs that would change the lives of countless Mexicans.

Antonio began by planning how we would help the people of the dump and the squatter communities. We agreed to organize a U. S. volunteer survey team to assess the most urgent needs for those living in the dump. We returned home to gather the survey team together.

Dr. Phyllis Cavens led the team of volunteers. She made survey sheets and sent the team in pairs with interpreters out into the dump. They tramped through the knee-high garbage to reach the people's shacks and ask the survey questions.

One of the volunteers, Carol Opsahl, shared her experience. She and her partner tried to reach a shack they had spotted ahead. Their path led them between two mountains of garbage. Carol squished through quagmire up to her ankles. They arrived at a shack and introduced themselves to a woman who met them at the door. Using the survey sheet, Carol asked whether there was a useable latrine. The lady looked at Carol with a funny expression, and replied, "Yes! You just walked through it."

The surveys were collected and the information analyzed. The results were plain. The people of the dump needed medical attention, food, clothing, education and the ability to bathe, especially for their infants and children. The needs of the squatter communities showed more of the same. We realized we had more work to do than we had planned.

Home Improvement

Suppose a brother or sister is without clothes and daily food. If one of you says to him, "Go, I wish you well; keep warm and well fed," but does nothing about his physical needs, what good is it? James 2:6

Antonio and I planned quickly. We first purchased an old

house next to the dump and called it the Community Center. Volunteer teams traveled to add rooms, paint, and make it attractive and functional. Showers were one of the first things built. It was an amazing experience to watch the children take their first shower. Nearly all of them had never had a bath in their lives. They lined up with excitement on their faces. Once inside, they smiled and laughed. They almost enjoyed the showers too much. Our volunteers had trouble moving each one out so others could get in the showers.

Cleanliness boosts our morale, I believe. In Biblical times, a person would always get up and wash after fasting or a time of deep depression. Washing was a sign that it was time to return to life again, and washing was the sign for these children to begin a new life — a life which held more hope of a future than the dump in which they lived.

A medical clinic was opened next. We had learned that all of the children had worms. The medical volunteers began treating the worm situation right away. A mother's health training class was also started to help prevent health problems in children.

Antonio started a breakfast feeding program that continues to this day. The children were only receiving one meal a day and sometimes went several days without food. Giving them a nutritional breakfast improved the children's concentration and comprehension, as well as their overall health.

All of these improvements required funds. For the first year and a half, I traveled to Mexico two weeks of every month, and then returned home for two weeks to raise the funds to do the work. When I was in Mexico, Antonio and I worked six days a week, averaging 15 hours a day, to make sure we had good programs. We worked well together. The combination of our personality traits mixed to make a phenomenal team, exuding enthusiasm, motivation and absolute tenacity to our goals. The rigorous schedule helped to develop a deep bond that we will have forever and, I will always cherish our close relationship.

In 1987, one year after we had begun our work with the people of the dump, the director of the ABC television program

"Good Morning America" (GMA) wanted to tell our story, declaring me as an "unsung hero." For NWMT, it was free advertising. The national attention would be an incredible opportunity.

The entire crew from GMA accompanied me to the Mexico City "Basurero" (dump). They all, including reporter Hattie Kaufman, slogged through it at my side. They stopped to record a scene that pictured a small child with a very dirty face, wearing little clothing, no shoes, and standing in a pile of chicken entrails. When the recording was finished, a camera operator put down his camera to weep. The producer cried, also. The producer later said, "We have reported on some very shocking and sad stories before, but we have never looked upon such poverty."

Another humiliation suffered by the dump inhabitants was that the public school system would not allow the "dump" children to attend the schools. The reasons included that the children were foul smelling, and could not afford books, uniforms and transportation, as other families. Thus, Antonio started a school at the community center where the children could learn reading, math and writing.

In 1994, an astounding feat was accomplished. Thanks to the gracious gift from Northwest Kiwanis Clubs and Harry Merlo of The Louisiana Pacific Foundation, a magnificent new school was built. Like a beacon of hope and guidance, Las Aguilas School was located on top of a hill overlooking the dump. Over 400 children could receive an education. Today, the school is the pride of the entire area for the people who live there. It has provided an opportunity for the children to take pride in themselves, to build their self-esteem, and to give them a hope for the future.

Other innovative ideas were worked into reality. For example, one of the most noticeable problems among the citizens of the dump was the lack of support from the men. Due to the dump's miserable living conditions, despair often overcame the husbands and fathers of the family structure. The men often left their families to look for work, and never returned. Others succumbed to alcoholism. Mothers and children were abandoned without any means of support.

In response, Antonio introduced the idea to begin an industrial sewing school. After completing the course, each woman would be able to secure jobs in the many textile factories around Mexico City, and thus support their families. With the stamp of approval from our board, and the financial support from home, many futures have been changed. Almost all of the ladies who lived in the dump have attended the school, graduated, and have improved their lives. The graduation ceremonies are extremely touching, because there is such a presence of hope in the auditorium, where there was no hope before.

One graduating student spoke eloquently to her graduating class about what the school meant to her. "Here I learned to walk each day of my life with Jesus Christ," she said. "Here I learned a skill that will greatly benefit my family. And here, I have gained self-worth."

After creating these "home improvements," we began to search for ways to develop "heart improvements." Our Mexican staff asked parents if they would allow their children to attend a Children's Bible Club program. The club was a place for their children to play, sing Christian songs, and learn from the Bible. Because of the trust and respect we had worked to obtain, many parents agreed to allow their children to attend.

The first Bible club began in the Las Aguilas dump with about 20 to 30 children. The clubs expanded to other areas in which we were helping, including the State of Oaxaca, Mexico. The number of clubs continued to grow to 30 or more with as many as 3,000 children attending weekly. A few of the clubs had as many as 400 children attending each week.

I believe that our Bible clubs were successful because of certain standards we set. First, it was important that the people's physical needs were met, before trying to feed them spiritually. Our good works were our initial witness of the love of Christ. In Matthew 5:16, Jesus said, "In the same way, let your light shine before men, that they may see your good deeds and praise your Father in heaven."

Another standard in which we believed was that our staff never tell the people which church they should attend. The purpose was to help them understand how to walk with God on a daily basis. Our Mexican and American staff attend many different Christian denominations, and this is expressed through all of our mission's endeavors.

One of the most important standards we set is that we never require anything in return for our services. From the beginning, no one has had to accept a tract, a Bible, listen to a sermon, or attend a Bible club in order to receive our help. Jesus never placed conditions on people. Why should we?

In 1998, twelve years after beginning the work in the dump, I was visiting the Bible club at the old community center. I met two sisters who first started attending the Bible club when they were five and six years old. One of them summarized what the improvements had meant to them: "The greatest thing that happened to us was to attend the Bible club where we began a close walk with God. Our father and our father's father knew only the work in the dump. We would have spent our lives doing the same, if we had not been involved in the program you have developed."

They both smiled, happily, and the other sister added, "We grew up taking showers at the community center, receiving a breakfast every morning, and participating in the education classes. When we completed elementary school at the center, you sponsored us to attend public high school, where a supporter in the United States paid for the yearly costs for books, uniforms and transportation. Now, we have completed high school. My sister has enrolled in nursing school, and I enrolled in the Industrial Sewing School. We have escaped the poverty of the dump. We will not grow old as "trash pickers."

The Las Aguilas dump ultimately closed down. We felt encouraged because we helped change lives and brought hope to these people. Our work there also served as an example for later endeavors to better the lives of "trash-pickers."

In 1995 we discovered another dump called Tulti, where people were living in the same conditions. We built a nice community center that will bring immense changes for these people as we did for those of Las Aguilas.

The Power of Teamwork

...make my joy complete by being like-minded, having the same love, being one in spirit and purpose. Philippians 2:2

The Las Aguilas Dump project was one of the most successful programs we have completed. Two sisters and hundreds more will not be "trash pickers," but have a more promising future than the life of the dump that their parents and grandparents have known. Many are working in textile factories now and there is a school to continue educating children for years to come. Children will no longer go hungry. Hundreds have placed their faith in God as a result of the developments started by NWMT.

The wonderful success in Mexico is due to ordinary people who worked together to accomplish extraordinary things. These volunteers did not question God, or accuse Him for creating such a mess, but instead answered God's call by saying, "Here I am, Lord," and, "I must do something." These people understood God's plan of helping others.

Ron Post holding a child in the dump in Mexico City. Photo, NWMT.

The donors who believed their sacrifice would make a difference; the prayers of caring supporters at home; the work teams who gave their time to build the community center, sewing school and elementary school; and the doctors and dentists who used their talents to heal were all essential elements in our outreach. The dedication of the American and Mexican staff was so amazing. They truly went "the extra mile" to see our vision become reality. The mission was also indebted to the Mexican people who went through our programs and then gave back by volunteering for them.

People from all sorts of backgrounds and representing many beliefs had compassion in their souls, and proved it with their actions. Accountants, insurance agents, truckers, contractors, teachers, plumbers, carpenters, beauticians, pastors, high school and college students, homemakers and many more professionals cared enough to "get up from their chairs" and expend their talents and money to help others. None of these people will be the same again. They all gained a sense of purpose and have become aware of who are "the least of these my brothers." Their experiences kindled a fire in their lives that will never be quenched.

I evaluated our success, and I treasured these thoughts in my heart. It is important to stop and celebrate our victories. These celebrations build our faith and help us overcome the hardships of later endeavors.

As I celebrated our mission's success, I looked back at how the goodness of God was shown to me through the hundreds of volunteers who cared for others. I remembered the volunteer who cared for a small, dirty child with puss running from her eyes. The deep concern was evident in his warm hug, and his soft voice as he spoke comfort to the child. Later, his eyes filled with tears as he described what this work meant to him.

It is sometimes difficult to understand true sacrifice for Christ when we live in such a prosperous nation. Our volunteers have no such problem, however. One team comes to my memory. They returned from a mountain village in Mexico where they helped the Indians install a clean water system in the village. They shared their excitement of helping the village rid itself of parasite-infected water. The children would no longer get sick from drinking the water. Yet, while reaching out to this village, they slept on the ground in tents with fleas biting all night. They worked in humid, heat digging ditches down mountainsides at 5,000 foot elevation that made their hearts pound and caused them difficulty in breathing. Most of them probably got diarrhea at some time during the week. When I reminded someone of this, her answer was, "Oh, it was worth it!" Another person said, "They helped us far more than we helped them." They understand the joy of sacrifice.

The outpouring of love and sacrifice of these volunteers caused me to look at myself. In prayer, I once again committed myself to God and told Him I was willing to deny myself and follow Him. I discovered that when I tell Him I am available, He is ready to answer. God was about to present us with the biggest undertaking to date.

CHAPTER SIX

THE FORGOTTEN PEOPLE

The liberal soul should be made fat: and he that watereth shall be watered also himself. Proverbs 11:25

"Ron, I've heard such good reports about the work your volunteer teams are doing in Mexico City. Would you come to Oaxaca and let me show you the Indians who live in the mountains and the tremendous difficulties they face?" asked Duane Marlow, the director of Mission Aviation Fellowship in Oaxaca, Mexico. It was the fall of 1986, and we had been working in Mexico City for a year when Duane made the call.

Duane explained the situation using statistics. "Oaxaca is 350 miles south of Mexico City. Overwhelming poverty is a fact of life for these people. The state of Oaxaca had 38% unemployment," he said, and added, "I have been flying people and supplies into the mountain Indian villages to help those who are severely sick and starving." The urgency in Duane's voice convinced me I should go. I promised him that on my next visit to Mexico, Antonio and I would visit him in Oaxaca.

Soon after Duane's call, Antonio and I flew to Oaxaca where Duane met us. The next morning, he flew us in a small plane to a village in the mountains. I had done my homework and read about Mission Aviation. They fly into the most remote areas of the world . As we flew, Duane explained how the Indians had carved out landing strips in many villages. Each tiny landing strip sat on the side of, or merely jutted out from, the mountain. Flying was the only way to reach the people unless we walked for several days, straight up a goat trail.

As we approached the village of Las Cuevas, Duane said,

"There it is."

I took a deep breath, and replied, "Are we really going to land on that?" It looked like a postage stamp. One end was embedded in the mountain and the other end jutted out over the vast valley below. A huge boulder blocked the end of the runway. It was the shortest landing strip I had ever seen.

When we were about 1000 feet out, Duane said, "We are now committed." Somehow, the word "committed" did not have the positive ring to it that it usually has. I grabbed the sides of my seat. My knuckles were white. We were flying at too high of an altitude to be able to land. I closed my eyes and said, "Lord into your hands I commit my soul."

Duane hit the end of the runway and we could see the huge rock at the other end. Immediately, he hit the brakes. The plane stopped about fifty feet before the rock. "Thank you, Lord, for landing us safely," I prayed. Apparently, one's perception can often play tricks in the mountains.

I could see the Indians of the village lined up at the edge of the runway, with curious faces. Duane shut the engine off and we got out of the plane. They were standing at a distance, and as we drew closer, I realized that I was not prepared for the experience before me.

Approximately 100 men, women and children greeted us. Most of the people were without shoes in the chilly mountain climate. Their clothing was torn and tattered, riddled with holes. It appeared as if they were wearing the only clothes they owned.

The state of the children was shocking. They looked like children I had seen in Ethiopia. Their bloated stomachs and reddish hair indicated malnutrition and/or parasites. However, these children were not across the entire world map, but were our next-door neighbors!

The questions I asked had startling answers. The people were growing corn and beans in the same manner they had been using for hundreds of years. They depended on rain to water their crops. The soil was poor after farming the same areas over the years, and because they had no fertilizers. It had been years since the rain had brought sufficient water, so the crops that did make it were never enough. After the corn and beans were eaten, the people had to forage for food, eating roots or whatever else they could find during those three to five months of the year. It had been another year of little rain, and they were very hungry.

The Indians were the forgotten people of Mexico. Medical facilities were unaccessible. Uneducated in how to prevent poor health, these people suffered greatly. No latrines existed. Their drinking water was drawn from a stream where laundry was washed, and animals waded through, adding their own urine and defecation. Many children were suffering from the contaminated water and lack of nutrition. All of them were hungry. They begged us to bring them food.

A small boy suffering from malnutrition caught Antonio's eye. His stomach was bloated, yet his body was thin and bony. I took a photograph of the boy because he seemed to represent the grave needs of the village. It hangs in Antonio's office to this day. Not long after visiting the village, the boy died. Antonio will never forget the boy. He remains in Antonio's memory and is a symbol of all who suffer.

We climbed into the airplane to take off, and the pain was evident in the people's faces. They needed so many things that it overwhelmed me. I prayed that our mission could make a difference.

Duane revved the engine up to nearly full throttle and released the brake. The rocky and bumpy runway rattled the plane so much that I wondered if the plane would fall apart. We approached the end of the runway that drops off into the huge valley. Duane had the stick pulled straight back, but the plane did not lift. I swallowed hard. We ran off the end of the runway without lifting off. My stomach jumped. We leapt into empty space and dropped toward the valley until the airspeed was sufficient to lift the plane.

After gaining altitude, my mind returned to the people of the village. I looked at Antonio and could sense that his heart had been touched. I think we both held back tears. As we flew over other villages on our way back to the capital of Oaxaca, Duane told me that many more mountain villages were in the same condition. He questioned, "Can you help?"

"Yes," I answered. Though we did not have the funds to begin such a work, I knew we had to try. To go home and ignore these sick and hungry people would be wrong.

When I returned, the board gathered for my proposal. After I shared the conditions of the Indians, they endorsed our desire to help and prayed for the financial support needed.

Letters were sent to our donors, describing the deplorable condition of these gentle people. They responsed generously. I called Antonio to tell him we could begin working.

Their greatest need was food. Duane agreed to fly sacks of corn, beans and rice to the villages. The flights continued for about six months until the new crops matured. The people often voiced their appreciation to Duane.

Next, we sent medical volunteer teams into the mountains. The volunteers would back-pack from village to village to treat the people for parasites and respiratory illnesses. The medical volunteers reported that dental problems were numerous. Many people suffered from abscesses and infections.

In response, we sent volunteer dental teams. The dental teams had an almost comical routine as they visited the villages. After arranging the people in a large circle, they began deadening the gums of each person, and then pulled the rotten teeth. The villagers were amazed at how quickly their pain ceased, and were very grateful. None of them had ever seen a dentist before.

Author and friend, John Duke, among Indian villagers. This village called La Humidad, in Oaxaca, Mexico, had never had North American Visitors. Photo, NWMT.

Dr. Richard Imholte, a dentist, was one of the volunteers to share a story with the audience at one of our fundraising banquets. The story illustrated the generosity of the forgotten people of Mexico.

"Like other teams, we would back-pack to different villages and pull teeth. After helping people at the first village, we were stunned by how many people came to say good-bye and bring gifts, such as eggs or maybe a chicken." Dr. Imholte paused, and continued, "Our team had come to the mountains well prepared. We certainly did not need food, especially from starving people. It was an awkward situation."

"Their offerings of food were probably all that they had. It was a sincere and genuine gift." Dr. Imholte noted, "We realized that refusing the gift would be considered extremely impolite, perhaps even insulting. Thus, we decided on a plan together. We accepted the food, but we took it with us to the next village, picked out the poorest family we could find, and gave the food to them." He smiled, and said, "This plan worked quite well for a while until we arrived at the last village."

"We had already given away the food given to us by the villagers, when we discovered a widow who had several children. She lived in the typical hut with a thatched roof, mud walls, and dirt floors. There was nothing on her shelves except for two eggs. We decided to give away the small amount of our own food that we had remaining. There was a half loaf of bread, a half box of pancake flour and a can of red hot peppers. Just scraps to us, but a feast to this woman. We left her little hut feeling happy about our good deed."

"We began walking toward the landing strip where a plane would pick us up. We had only walked about fifty feet when we heard the widow's voice. We turned. The widow stood a few feet from us with her hand stretched out. She was holding her two eggs." Dr. Imholt stopped, and allowed a small silence to pervade the room. "We did not know what to do. We were going home where there were plenty of eggs. The widow desperately needed them. We looked at each other with tears in our eyes."

The dentist stopped his narrative there, and sat down deliberately. In the midst of the silence, a question was whispered to each of the members of the audience. "What would you have done?"

I have often remembered that story and wondered what I would have done. I admired the widow. One day, perhaps Jesus will commend her as he did another widow in Luke 21:1-4. "As he looked up, Jesus saw the rich putting their gifts into the temple treasury. He also saw a poor widow put in two very small copper coins. 'I tell you the truth,' he said, 'this poor widow has put in more than all the others. All these people gave their gifts out of their wealth; but she out of her poverty put in all she had to live on.'"

Following the dentists' outreach, health promoters were chosen from each village. They learned how to grow vegetables year-round, which would give them a more balanced diet. They also learned basic medical care and preventative health care. Then they returned to their villages and taught the other villagers what they had learned. This program has reduced malnutrition and improved health in many of the villages.

We also sent teams to work alongside villagers to install clean water systems in the villages. Eighty percent of illnesses disappeared as a result. Other teams built latrines and worked on other improvements. The outreach continues today because there are so many villages in need.

When we said yes to God's plans, He allowed us to participate in the joy of giving. We not only helped the village where Antonio and I first visited, but also hundreds of communities in the mountains of Oaxaca. When God is in charge of the plan, the successes are abundant.

The Outcasts
Hope deferred maketh the heart sick: but when the desire cometh, it is a tree of life. Proverbs 13:12

In 1987, Antonio and I met with a Mexican plastic surgeon, Dr. Caesar Mayoral. Dr. Mayoral described another immense problem in Oaxaca. "Approximately 5000 children suffer from cleft lip and palates," he stated, "but there are not enough doctors to perform the surgery to correct them." He added, "My brother and I are the only plastic surgeons in the state. Although we have performed some surgeries for which we did not charge, we cannot begin to do all of them."

"Why are there so many?" I asked.

"In my opinion," Dr. Mayoral answered, "it is because these people live in small villages and have inter-married over the years. A genetic problem has developed as a result. I often see two or three people with a cleft palate within the same family." He added, "Some children die early because of a hole in the palate that does not allow them to suck milk."

"How sad, and unnecessary," I thought. Children in the United States can have the malformation taken care of in infancy. Most insurances cover the corrective surgery for a cleft palate, or the family can receive help from the government.

Dr. Caesar explained that children with this problem in Oaxaca are hidden away in huts as outcasts. Some connect it to a religious belief considered to be a punishment from God. "The children are not allowed to play with other children, go to school or consider marriage," he said, noting that many of the children continue into their elderly years with this health and societal dilemma.

"Can you send teams of plastic surgeons to help?" Dr. Mayoral asked. "It would significantly change the lives of so many."

"Yes," I answered. I strongly believed that God would want us to do all we could for these hidden children.

One of the obstacles to overcome was where to perform the surgeries. It would be difficult to do them in Mexican hospitals, where space and equipment were limited. Again, I had no idea what would be needed. However, I did know we had enthusiastic people at home who would help me find the answers to my questions.

I returned home and picked up the telephone. Despite my family members who have often teased me by saying a permanent telephone grows from my car, the telephone has been the perfect tool for accomplishing God's plans. After conferencing with Dr.

Jerry Becker and Jim Bowlin, medical volunteers from the El Salvador earthquake, we crafted in our minds a van that could be converted into an operating room. Jim said that he and Jerry owned a fifth-wheel trailer. They offered it to store the medical supplies. We soon found a truck that had just come down from Alaska. Though it was old, it had a new engine and it was kept in excellent condition.

I was becoming weary by this time. For over a year, I had been working on the schedule of two weeks in Mexico, and two weeks at home. During the two weeks home, I spent time fundraising. Facing this new project made me feel weak inside. I could sense that burn-out was peeking around the corner.

I prayed about it, and God answered. A man named Doug Rawlins came into my office one day to ask questions about his church becoming involved with our mission. Through our conversation, I learned that he and his wife Pam had spent time in Guatemala working in Indian villages for the Peace Corp. After I discovered that he and Pam were fluent in Spanish, I realized I was speaking to my opportunity. Before he left my office that day, I asked him to consider coming on staff to run the work in Mexico. Doug went home and consulted with his wife. Pam said, "Doug, if you do not take that job, I will!"

Doug called me and said, "Yes, I will do it." Doug became a faithful fellow laborer in God's harvest field, as well as a genuine friend. His work in Mexico has been productive and diligent. He truly was an answer to prayer.

Doug's first job was to coordinate the conversion of the truck van into an operating room. He enlisted the help of some local volunteers who did the carpentry and installed the medical equipment. Several of our volunteers drove the truck and fifth-wheel trailer over 3,000 miles to Oaxaca.

One day, Doug received a call from Dr. Bob Demuth, the director of plastic surgery for Oregon Health Science University in Portland, Oregon. Dr. Demuth said, "I've heard about Mexico's need for plastic surgeons. Can I help?"

God is faithful. Like an angel of the Lord, Dr. Demuth came equipped with instructions for the steps we needed to take. After he and Doug decided the procedure and list of materials for the medical teams, they recruited medical people for the work. Dr. Demuth then volunteered to lead the team to Mexico. He traveled many times with out teams to Mexico and other countries in need, performing surgeries for NWMT.

For three years we operated out of the back of the van and our teams performed hundreds of corrective surgeries on children with cleft lip and palates. What a dramatic change occurred after

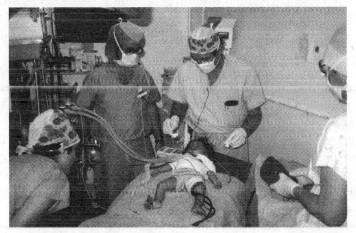

Dr. Bob Demuth, right, prepares to perform a cleft lip and palate surgery on an Indian child. Photo, NWMT.

that simple hour and a half surgery! It seemed as if the van was a crysalis where caterpillars were transformed into butterflies. The children left with wings to fly — they would no longer be hidden in huts, but could play and live as other children.

A young couple brought their two-month-old son who had a cleft lip and palate to our van. Their eyes sad and afraid, as they asked whether their child could be helped. They wanted their son to be like other children. An hour and a half later, the young couple's faces had changed completely. Smiles of hope and joy spread across their faces as they looked into their child's face.

A year later, the couple had another child with the same problem and we corrected it. I had the pleasure of meeting the family again. The children are involved in school and are participating in activities like other children. The parents told us how grateful they were to us for giving their children a better future.

One day, a man brought his 14-year-old daughter to the surgical van. She had what is called a bi-lateral cleft lip. This means she had no upper lip except for a small piece below the nose. The father confessed to us how ashamed he felt. "I believe I must have offended God," he said. "Perhaps I should have behaved differently."

The team performed the surgery, and it was successful. A year and a half later, I saw the girl walking with her father. She was now 16, and blossoming into a young lady. She looked wonderful! Though still shy, her pleasure at her countenance was easily observed. Her father was so proud. With a wide smile on his face, he told us she was in the eighth grade and doing well. "Now, she will be able to marry and have a happy life," he exclaimed.

We also performed many surgeries on people in their later years of life. One man in his sixties came to the van for surgery. When the surgery was over, a nurse gave him a mirror. He looked into the mirror and his eyes widened, as he said, "Oh, now I can take a wife!"

We all laughed and cried. We were happy because a life had been changed, yet we were saddened that the life wasn't changed sooner. A lot of years of pain had been experienced by the man. In my thoughts, I whispered the words, "If only..." and then stopped. There is no "if only" with God; the past and future is always overwhelming and can paralyze what we can do in the present. I was grateful for the good that had been accomplished. I thanked God that I could be a part of it.

The Blind

...he has annointed me to preach good news to the poor. He has sent me to proclaim freedom for the prisoners and recovery of sight for the blind, to release the oppressed ... Isaiah 61:1,2

A few years after we started repairing cleft lip and palates, another tragedy was brought to our attention. Thousands of elderly Indians were blind or going blind from cataracts. No surgery was available to these people, and thus, they resigned themselves to never seeing again. Becoming blind was extremely devastating because no retirement plans, social security or Medicare were available. Because each family member con tributes to support the family by weaving, sewing, cooking, and planting, they believe their usefulness is gone when they go blind. They often feel they are no longer worthy to be part of the family.

Antonio, Doug, and I discussed the problem. Since the surgery truck was already located in Oaxaca, we felt it was possible to provide help to these people.

The author encouraging one of fifteen elderly Indians who was blind the day before. The average person had been blind from cataracts for three years. Photo courtesy of NWMT.

Doug recruited Dr. Roger David and Dr. Bill Pendergast of Oregon City, Oregon, to advise him on the procedure to begin a program to remove cataracts. The doctors helped Doug develop a plan, as well as gather the supplies. The two eye surgeons also led the first team to operate out of the truck. They would blaze the trail which many teams would follow.

Both our plastic and eye surgery teams kept costs down to $137 per person. This was amazingly low, considering what it would cost in the United States. Teamwork was the key. The medical teams donated their professional time and paid for their travel, lodging and meals. The surgical supplies were donated. A group of individuals can accomplish far more working together, than each working alone. Hundreds of pairs of eyes see again, due to the teamwork of all who volunteered time or money to help the Indians restore their sight.

It is so exciting to be present on the day an eye patch is removed. Watching a blind person see his or her relatives for the first time in years is a phenomenal experience. We all weep. Though I have seen this marvelous event many times, it never becomes routine.

There have been many stories like that of Fredrico, who had been blind for twenty years. His son had led him by hand into our clinic for the surgery. When the bandage was removed, the doctor asked Fredrico, "Can you see?"

Fredrico paused and said, "Yes, I see people in front of me!"

Then, his son stepped in front of Fredrico. The doctor asked, "Do you know this man?"

Fredrico stared at the man, and replied, "No." The father had not seen his son in twenty years. When he last saw him, he was a boy of fourteen years.

The son spoke, and Fredrico exclaimed, "It's my son!" We all laughed and cried as the miracle unfolded before us.

God's Hands

I tell you the truth, anyone who has faith in me will do what I have been doing. He will do even greater things than these, because I am going to the Father. And I will do whatever you ask in my name, so that the Son may bring glory to the Father. John 14:12-13

These verses have confused me in the past. How could we do greater deeds than those of Jesus? He fed more than 5,000 people from a few loaves of bread and a couple of fish. He healed the sick, gave sight to the blind, and made the lame walk.

After the outreach to the Indians, the Lord opened my eyes and helped me to understand the verses. Jesus touched a few pairs of eyes, and they were healed. However, the sight of hundreds of blind individuals has been restored through our outreach. Thousands of sick have been healed from the efforts of our teams. The key phrases to which we must give attention are "anyone who has faith in me" and "ask in my name."

I asked the Lord to help us reach out to the Mexican people, to those who lived in the dump and squatter communities, and to the forgotten Indians in the mountains of Oaxaca. I asked in Jesus' name that the seemingly overwhelming tasks would be made possible.

God answered by touching the hearts of many people. Many provided funds, time, and effort. All of these people were the "anyone who has faith," and through our combined efforts, God produced more miracles than Christ performed while on earth. Jesus' words ring true today.

A statue of Jesus stood in front of a church in San Diego, California. One morning, people discovered that vandals had broken the hands off the statue. Shaking their heads, the people made plans to repair the damage done. However, the next morning, someone propped a sign up against the statue that read, "I have no hands but your hands."

We are Jesus' hands! Since we are the Christ's hands, we should use them as He would — reaching out to the poor and suffering. The Lord loves every person on this earth and grieves when they hurt. He gave us the greatest example he could by caring for their needs.

Many people have caught the vision of being His hands to those in need. Because they have reached out, there are fewer hungry and sick people in our world. God has a promise for those who have compassion on others. Proverbs 19:17 reads, "He who is kind to the poor lends to the Lord, and he will reward him for what he has done."

The Rewards of Service

He who is kind to the poor lends to the Lord, and he will reward him for what he has done. Proverbs 19:17

In 1994, I was awarded the Kiwanis World Service Medal in New Orleans. The medal was created in 1985 as a means for Kiwanis International to recognize individuals whose dedication to altruistic services can serve as an inspiring example to others. In the past, the medal, which is awarded once a year, has been given to such notable people as Nancy Reagan and Audrey Hepburn. The award also carries a $10,000 grant which was turned over to the mission. It was a wonderful opportunity to represent all those who give to others.

It was a deep-felt honor to receive the award from such a respected group. Kiwanis International represents civic clubs around the world doing "good works" for people who are in need.

Jean and I attended the event together. Before the ceremony, we spent some time in prayer to ask God to bless the event. Our prayer was simple; we asked that Jesus would receive the glory.

Nearly 13,000 people were seated in the huge convention center. Over a hundred countries were represented. At first sight of the huge crowd, I said to Jean, "Honey, let's go back to our room!" It was frightening to think that I would soon be standing in front of all these people in a few moments, and expected to speak. Jean, in her usual way, said, "You will be fine." Then, she reminded me, "Give God the glory."

The President of Kiwanis International gave a message. Then, a short video of Northwest Medical Teams was shown. As the video ended, I was at the back of the stage. My pulse quickened when the president said, "Please welcome the 1994 Kiwanis World Service Medal recipient, Dr. Ronald Post." As I walked to the front, the sea of people stood to their feet to applaud. I shook the president's hand (mine was sweaty) and then stepped to the podium.

"Wow — your response is really humbling and this check is really wonderful," I said. "I want to first offer this award to the Lord Jesus Christ as a gift of praise. Secondly, I wish to acknowledge that this medal and most generous check are received as a direct result of the thousands of medical and lay volunteers who have given of their time and their resources to serve the world's poorest. I think of our wonderful staff, our local volunteers, and our board of directors whose combined skills have made us what we are today."

All the people erupted in applause and stood up. I tried to fight back the tears, for I could feel the presence of God standing there beside me. I stood there with my eyes lifted to heaven as they applauded and silently said, "This is for you, Lord!"

Later, I took time to reflect on the event. I have never owned Northwest Medical Teams. It is owned by God and operated by many ordinary, but wonderful, people who serve the poor. Thus, I felt very little ownership of the award. The praise belonged to God and to all those who have worked so hard to make a difference in our world. I stood in merely as their representative. It belongs to all who act as God's hands.

CHAPTER SEVEN

SEARCHING FOR HOME

I have come down...to bring them...into a good and spacious land, a land flowing with milk and honey. Exodus 3:8

After several years, our outreach to Mexico became more settled. We decided on a name, "Manos de Ayuda," which means "Helping Hands," and Antonio Vazquez became the president of the agency.

Medical teams continued to perform surgeries out of the truck van. When the van was not in use, it was parked in front of a building which we rented to use as a clinic. A Mexican doctor was hired to run the clinic to care for the poor in a community of St. Augustine, located about three miles from the city of Oaxaca.

The building was also used as a school to train people from the mountain villages about health issues. Once trained, the person would return to his village to teach and provide health care to those who lived in his community. Other people from the same villages would come to learn mini-gardening techniques so they could grow vegetables year-round, which would improve their health immensely.

The success of this approach soon brought another obstacle. The building was not large enough to hold more students. Also, many more patients needed surgeries, which would require more rooms. It became increasingly clear that we could not perform any more cases than we were doing with only the operating room within the truck van.

If we could purchase about three acres of land, we could build a surgery center as well as a school for health and agriculture students. The acreage would provide enough room to grow demonstration gardens to show students the correct methods for mini-gardening. As usual, we did not have the funds to undertake such a project, yet the importance of such a center was obvious. It would enable us to serve so many more of the poor in Oaxaca.

I asked Antonio if he would begin looking around the city for properties. I figured we could purchase three acres around the city for about $6000. However, I was wrong. Antonio called and said that property around the city was running $30,000 an acre! Many Americans were coming to Oaxaca to retire, and this was driving up the prices. I realized that to buy three acres and build the buildings we needed would require far too much money. After more discussion, we decided to have Antonio look for one-acre properties, though the fit would be tight.

A few days later, Antonio called and said that he had located a number of properties for us to view. It was arranged that Doug Rawlins, Fred Kerns, who was helping get our village water projects going, and myself to fly there.

We arrived in the evening. The next morning, Antonio escorted us to different one-acre properties. Each time we would walk onto a piece of land, all of us had the same response. We just did not feel as if this was the property we should have. One property was located right next to the airport, which seemed like an ideal place to build. Yet, still it did not feel right. We questioned ourselves: should we trust feelings and turn each one down?

We became discouraged when we realized that we had viewed all of the properties near the city. Then, Antonio said, "Senior, there is another piece at which we can look, but it's twenty miles outside the city."

I thought, "Twenty miles away is much too far. Why would we want a place that far from the city?" However, I said nothing about it, and agreed to view the property. Antonio had gone to the trouble of finding these properties. The least we could do was to look at them.

We all got into the van and drove the twenty miles. It seemed as if we were in the middle of nowhere. The landscape looked like high desert. Finally, we turned off the main road and went about a half mile down a dirt road. Antonio stopped the van and began to outline the property line by the tree and brush rows.

I said, "Antonio, this must be twenty acres!"

"No Senior, it's thirty acres," he replied.

I thought, "What are we doing here? If we could not afford three acres, how could we even think about thirty?"

"There is a well on the property. Would you like to see it?" Antonio asked.

"Sure," I answered. Once again, I felt I should honor Antonio's efforts to find the property. We drove the van out to the middle of the property where the well was located. The water was just eighteen feet below the ground, which was surprising since the terrain was desert.

Fred Kern said, "The well would certainly provide enough water."

Yet, my mind could not see beyond the price of thirty acres. How could we ever afford a place like this? When we had turned off the main road, Antonio had pointed out a two-acre parcel which was priced at $40,000. I was getting impatient. There

The author holding some thorns and reminding Antonio Vazquez of the time they stood in a circle of men to praise the Lord for his suffering. That brought about the Surgery Center Property seen in the background. Photo, NWMT.

94

seemed to be no point in looking at a place which was impossible for us to buy.

Holy Ground
Take off your sandals, for the place where you are standing is holy ground.
Exodus 3:5

As we had driven to view the well, I had seen many holes dug in the ground. Being a former construction contractor, I became curious about them, and wondered what their purpose was. As our group examined the well, I walked over to examine the holes more closely. I asked Antonio to pick me up on the way out.

I walked to the other side of the property and realized that the holes were dug in order to pull up some of the thorny tree-like plants that grow there. As I was kneeling on one knee looking down into a hole, something lying by my foot caught my eye. I reached down and picked up a twig about nine inches long, which had long thorns pointing up and down it.

As I held it, I was suddenly impacted with the memory of the thorns our Savior once had to wear on His head. I felt the points of the thorns. They were like needles that could easily pierce your skin. A long time ago, Roman soldiers had taken the same type of twigs and had woven them together to form a crown, shoving them down on the Lord's head. I imagined the pain of the thorns penetrating his skin, and the discomfort of the blood streaming down his head and filling his eyes.

How little those soldiers knew of the One on whom they placed the thorns. The man they attempted to humiliate was the Son of God. How easy it would have been for Him to call down 10,000 angels to rescue Him.

Yet, the Lord endured the pain for the soldiers who abused him, and the officials who condemned him, and for all those who had ever been and whoever would come. He endured it for the whole world.

He also endured it for me. I was not worthy of this great sacrifice and yet he did it in spite of my sin and weaknesses.

Tears filled my eyes and ran down my face. A love for the Lord
Jesus welled up within me. I thanked him for the great sacrifice
he made for me. The field in which I was standing became a
sanctuary. I unashamedly praised God. I could feel his presence
and love in a very special way. I wanted to wrap my arms around
Him and tell Him how much I loved Him and how thankful I was
for the life He was willing to give up for me. Joy filled my heart
and I wanted to shout it out to the world.

The group had finished looking at the well and drove the
van over to where I was. They stopped, and everyone walked over
to where I stood. I told them about my experience. Then, I said,
"I don't know why we have come to this property, nor what the
Lord's plans are, but I feel as if we should spend time praising
Him." I paused, and continued. "Let's form a circle and hold
hands."

Each person began praising the Lord. Soon, we were all
weeping. We lifted our voices to the Lord, as time seemed to stand
still. It was one of the greatest experiences of my life. I felt so
close to the Lord. We were standing on holy ground.

God's Response
"He inhabits the praise of Israel." Psalm 22:3

We returned to the van. As we drove away, Antonio asked
whether I wanted to speak to the seller of the property.
Something inside me said we should. We drove back to the city
and went to visit the owner, a Mexican doctor. As we talked, we
learned that he was married to a Spanish woman. She had
become homesick and returned to Spain. He was clearing up his
affairs so he could join her.

Antonio asked him how much he wanted for the property.
The man thought for a few seconds, and said, "Would $16,000 be
too much?"

Antonio answered, "You mean an acre?"

The doctor replied, "No, I mean for the thirty acres."

When Antonio translated this for us, I looked at Doug. The
doctor must have thought we were crazy because we started to

cry. I did not hesitate. "Yes, we will take it!"

We were all in agreement. The Lord was providing the property, and this was the place to build our center. With joy in our hearts, we left the doctor's office, and spent time thanking the Lord for the miracle.

The experience taught me how much God loves our praise. He even responds to our needs through our praise. I had always known God loved our praise, but I thought when it came to our needs, we should always ask through prayer. I had never thought of our Lord meeting our needs through our praise.

It makes sense now. I respond to people who give me praise. Through my children and grandchildren, I discovered that when I praise them, they responded positively. All of us like and need praise. God also responds to my praise, for it is an expression of my love for Him.

God does know our needs before we ask Him. He directed Antonio to the property, and he directed me to the thorns. We thought we needed three acres of land, but God wanted us to have thirty.

One
I am only one,
But still I am one,
I cannot do everything,
But still I can do something;
And because I cannot do everything
I will not refuse to do the something that I can do.
Edward Everett Hale

I returned to the United States in an excited frame of mind. Though there were still not enough funds to build, I had no doubt that they would be provided. Confidently, I waited for the "how" and "when" to be answered. "If" did not even enter into my mind.

I sent out letters which explained to donors about the plan, asking them to support the project. Help was also sought from the people who attended our banquets, but we came up short.

I believed so strongly that the money would come, I authorized Antonio to buy the land and begin construction. To begin construction without the funds is not good business sense. Yet, trust was growing in my heart. Many times, steps of faith do not make much business sense, but they must be taken just the same.

Antonio was having his faith tested as well, as we tried to raise funds. Convincing his staff that building twenty miles outside the city was the right thing to do was not an easy task. Plenty of objections found paths to Antonio's ears. Some said that people would not be able to reach the center because it was too far away. Others did not want to travel that far to work. Patiently, Antonio reminded them that the Lord had chosen the spot, and when God is in control, everything falls into place.

The answer to our financial needs would be met in an unlikely way. It was March, 1990, and somewhere in Seattle, Washington, God was working on a unique idea. The story was covered by local television stations and newspapers. Erik Lacitis, a reporter for the Seattle Times, wrote one of them as follows:

"A few months ago, Monte Clouston, 35, decided what his mission would be. He had been feeling burned out. He wanted a change. He wanted to help do something good.

Clouston decided he would get a house built and sell it. He would then turn over the profits to a fund for constructing a hospital in one of Mexico's poorest regions. It is the state of Oaxaca, populated mostly by Indian's.

Clouston had visited that impoverished area, where volunteer doctors perform surgery in a converted moving van. He had watched a beggar woman break into tears when given some left-over steak dinner from a restaurant.

That would be his mission: to help the Indian villagers. I'm sure that charitable groups are quite familiar with proposals such as this. A well-meaning individual trying to help comes up with a grand idea for raising money. Unfortunately, reality soon makes its unpitying appearance. After costs, the group might end up with a piddling amount of money. They'd have been better off with a $5 check from everybody at the office.

But here was Monte Clouston saying he was going to get all

these volunteers and all this donated material, and build this three-bedroom, 2 1/2-bathroom, cathedral-ceiling, marble-entryway house.

The charitable group that Clouston wanted to help was Northwest Medical Teams, out of Portland. Its doctors have, in some cases, provided the only medical help that villagers in remote areas of Oaxaca receive.

Before telling you how Clouston's mission ended, a little background on him. At an obviously early age, he decided to become an entrepreneur. After college, he sold real estate for a couple of years. Then he concluded that it wasn't the career for him.

'So I bought a chunk of land, hired kids from my church, and started building houses,' Clouston said. Clouston earned tidy profits from apartment buildings he built, but he also burned out. It seemed to him he was always fighting city officials, or somebody, on something. Especially nowadays, as our last farmlands are taken over by rampant housing sprawls, developers are not exactly admired.

'Some neighbor gets mad because you're building on the vacant lot where he walks his dog,' Clouston said. 'Well, he could have bought that lot, but now he's complaining that you're blocking his view.'

That's when a friend's wife told Clouston about the medical teams. Clouston checked it out. Maybe there was some way he could help. He paid his own way to Oaxaca to watch the group's work. 'When you see a little girl who burned her hand in a fire, and I mean her two little fingers were burned so you could see bone, and she had to hike for two days for help...,' Clouston said. He knew he had to build the house. He began making phone calls and writing letters.

Balser Investments donated at cost a lot at a Martha Lake development. Parker Paints gave the paint for free, Hillsdale Pozzi came through with all the home's doors, and on and on. Individuals such as Ruben Peck, a hotel maintenance engineer, donated time in the actual construction. Clouston never had to do much selling on his project with the suppliers, perhaps because he was so obviously passionate about it.

He didn't just put together the list of volunteers. He has helped build the home himself, especially when he has run short of donated labor.

Last weekend the house was sold for $145,000, even though it needs finishing work. It's a hot real estate market in Puget Sound. Clouston estimates the profit to be $80,000. 'It's kind of amazing. I've never worked so hard as I am now for free,' Clouston said. 'I don't think I've had a weekend off since May.'

After this project, Clouston still has one more mission in Oaxaca. On November 1, he'll be part of a group of volunteers paying their own way, about $1000 each, to fly there and spend two weeks building the hospital. About all that Monte Clouston, who took a little time off from the rat race to help, can tell you is: 'When I was down there, the things I saw moved me so much. I'll never be the same again.' "

Endurance

Do you not know that in a race all the runners run, but only one gets the prize? Run in such a way as to get the prize. I Corinthians 9:24

The article motivated many people when it appeared. Monte gave up unbelievable amounts of time to build the house, but Monte had a vision. He saw what a surgical clinic could accomplish in bringing healing to many for years to come.

Monte and all the volunteers had tremendous endurance and strong faith to complete the project. Each had to support their families during the long construction period; thus, they had to give up week nights and weekends to complete the job. They grew tired at times, for it was a difficult trip to the construction site. Monte said that concentrating on the rewards of giving was what kept him going. "We had a mission and had to keep our focus on the end result," Monte said. "We had to keep reminding ourselves what this project would accomplish in the lives of those Indians."

Monte's example of endurance was an amazing witness. Endurance is something I wanted so that I would never be overwhelmed by my tasks. With it, I can accomplish great things. With God's strength, I might find the determination to stay the course, and through a strong, steady pace, I will finish the race I

The author and Elias Betanzos (far left) with a pastor and his wife who had received a new concrete floor for their tiny home. Elias directs all operations in Mexico. Photo, NWMT

began so many years ago. Though the course has been grueling at times, I am determined to win the prize — Christ will hand me a crown that will not tarnish and say, "Well done, thou good and faithful servant." With determination, all of us can be winners.

Monte and his friends ran a wonderful race, and they endured to the finish line. Monte is one of the finest examples of what one individual can do. He showed us by his example that each of us can make a difference. Some talk about it, some dream about it, but Monte did it!

The money Monte raised in the sale of the house made it possible to complete the surgical center, school building, dormitory and dining hall on the property. The campus is beautiful. Everyone who sees it is pleased.

The location has not deterred people from coming. At the old clinic, we would see about thirty people a day. The first day we opened the new clinic, we had the same amount of patients arrive, and the number grew as word went out. It now has nearly 200 people who show up daily!

Many more surgeries are performed than before because we built two operating rooms in the surgery center. The Mexican medical staff see people every day for many types of illnesses. A dental clinic was also opened.

We ask patients for a nominal fee. However, no one is turned away. The fee helps to maintain the patient's dignity and also provides for our Mexican medical staff. Though the staff had originally resisted the new clinic, they trusted what Antonio told them. Now, they speak of the grounds with great pride, and enjoy working there. Our staff is such a blessing. It consists of compassionate people who work hard for a small salary, and they do it because they want to serve their people.

Suffering for His Glory

I consider that our present sufferings are not worth comparing with the glory that will be revealed in us. Romans 8:18

By 1992, our mission in Mexico had greatly increased. We realized that it was getting too large for our director, Antonio. Running the programs in Mexico City, as well as the Oaxaca programs 350 miles south, was more than we could ask of the dedicated and hard-working man. Someone was needed to direct the work in Oaxaca.

Back in 1987, Antonio introduced a shy, young man to me. Elias Betanzos was working as the accountant for our Mexico City office. He spoke no English, so our conversation had to be translated through Antonio. Later, I learned that he was attending seminary school on the side and was working towards becoming ordained. I was glad that we could provide employment for him to become a pastor. Elias worked in the office for a number of years, quietly doing his job. Then he left our work to pastor a church in the state of Chiapas around 1990. At the time, I did not fully understand why he left. It would be years later before I knew.

Sometime after asking Antonio to find a director for the mission in Oaxaca, he called and said, "I have just the right person to direct the work in Oaxaca — Elias Betanzos."

I responded, "Antonio, I know Elias did a great job for you in Mexico City as your accountant, but are you sure he will make a good leader? Anyway, isn't he a pastor of a church in Chiapas now? "

Antonio answered, "Yes, Senior, he is. However, in school he studied administration. I would like to ask him if he would consider this position. Elias would do an excellent job as the director of the work in Oaxaca." Antonio knew this quiet man more than I did, so I agreed to his plan. Later, Antonio called me to say Elias had accepted the position.

Elias showed that Antonio was correct. He is a competent leader who receives respect from the staff in Oaxaca. Quiet leadership is not ineffective — a point which Elias has proven. His excellence in leadership has shown in how he runs the existing programs in Oaxaca, as well as how he responds to new programs. He is quick to take the initiative, and understands his authority to make decisions when needed. For example, when Mexico was struck by overpowering hurricanes in Oaxaca several times, Elias responded by forming a medical team from his staff. He organized relief supplies and rallied individuals and churches to help in the effort. His dedication and example inspired his staff, and many others, to give to those in need.

Just recently, Elias shared his journey to become the leader of our Oaxaca outreach. I had no idea up until that time the struggle he had been through. His story was so moving, and revealed so vividly the sincere and dedicated heart of Elias, that I want to share it here.

"I grew up in the southernmost state of Mexico called Chiapas. It borders the country of Guatemala, and the majority of people live in extreme poverty. My father was a pastor, and was so poor he could not afford to buy his children shoes and many times had to send them to school without breakfast. I vowed I would never live like that. I never wanted to be a pastor and be poor like my father.

"I went to school and studied administration. Not wanting to stay in Chiapas and risk poverty, I sought work in Mexico City. However, my father had committed my life to Jesus, and he felt that I was going to be greatly used by God. This was hard for me to imagine since I wanted no part of the life my father had lived.

"However, after securing a job with Manos de Ayuda as an accountant, I felt it would be all right to attend a seminary school in Mexico City. This would bring joy to my father, whom I loved and respected. The schedule was difficult. At 4:30 a.m. I would get up and prepare to leave for seminary school. At 1 p.m., I left the school

Children praying at one of thirty Bible Clubs that meet weekly in Mexico.
Photo, NWMT

for the office where I would work until 7 p.m., sometimes 8 p.m.

"When I graduated, I was asked to take over as pastor of a church in Mexico City. At first, I fought the idea. Then, I realized that it would be a safe step since I had a good job with Manos de Ayuda. Once again, I felt that by accepting the call, I would be honoring my father.

"The church only had about twenty-five people, but it soon grew to an attendance of about 250 people. Because I was receiving salaries from both the church and Manos de Ayuda, I could now afford to buy things I never thought possible. Being married with children, I could buy them nice things. My future seemed secure. I would never have to experience as a man, what I did as a child.

"God's ways are not our ways. One day, some people approached me who were from the state of Chiapas, and asked me to pastor their church. When they told me about the church, I discovered that only twenty-five elderly people attended. The people said they felt sure that I was the man God wanted there.

"I, on the other hand, was sure that I did not want to be there. I quickly declined. Why in the world would I ever want to do such a thing? I had two secure jobs, and could comfortably support my family. To move would be unwise!

Yet, inside my heart the turmoil began. The Holy Spirit would not let me rest, because he was urging me to go. I asked God, 'Why would you have me do this, Lord? I don't understand. I am serving you at the church here, as well as at Manos de Ayuda. What more could you want?'

"Still, I could not lose the idea that God wanted me to go to Chiapas. I desire to obey God, and to be where God wants me to be. In the end, the quiet voice of the Holy Spirit won in my heart. I told the people from Chiapas that I would accept. I did not understand it, but I obeyed. Though it seemed foolish, I trusted that God had a bigger plan than I could fathom.

"I arrived in Chiapas to find a small church with a mud house for me and my family. Creatures were crawling all over the place when we entered. My family was very courageous in the midst of these changes. I began the work I felt God wanted me to do. The church soon grew to ninety people.

"Though the church succeeded, my own personal finances dwindled. After more than a year, I had returned to the same state of poverty from which I had tried to escape as a boy.

"Then, Antonio called me. He asked how I was doing, and before long in telling him, I was in tears. I told him how my daughter had recently needed shoes. When I gathered all of my money, I found that I only had thirty pesos ($3.50). We went to town and searched, but we could not find a pair of shoes for that price. I was reminded of the times when my own father could not afford shoes for me. I remembered the vow I had made to never allow this to happen to me. A rush of pain and embarrassment filled my soul, and I sat down on the curb and wept. I cried out to God, 'Why have you brought me to this place of poverty?'

"Sometime later, a number of larger churches began offering me positions. One church was located where my wife's parents lived. We visited the church, and later accepted the position. Hope sprung up in our hearts. We could make more money and live near relatives.

"However, as we traveled home, the Holy Spirit once again began to convict my spirit. The quiet voice seemed to be telling me not to go. It became so strong that by the time we arrived, I called the church, asked for forgiveness, and declined the position. I returned to the little church in Chiapas.

"When Antonio called with the offer to direct the work in Oaxaca, I knew better than to accept right away. Instead, I laid a fleece before the Lord. I prayed, "Lord, I will take this position only if I am offered a position as pastor of a church in Oaxaca."

"I continued to serve the church and my community, but my poverty grew even worse. Finally, to provide for my family, I was forced to put up for sale the last vestige of my past — my old car.

"One day, four people approached my little mud home. Believing they came to look at the car, I walked out and began to tell them about it. One of the people interrupted, "We have not come to buy your car. We are from Oaxaca. We have come to ask you to be the pastor of our church." I could not believe it! I had never met these people, nor visited their church. I knew they were an answer from the Lord."

Elias and his family moved to Oaxaca, and Elias pastored the church. The church grew from ten people to over 200 today. He preached on Sundays, and worked as director of the outreach of Manos de Ayuda during the week. Under his leadership, the Children's Bible Clubs grew from ten to twenty in one year. By 1999, over 3,000 children attended the weekly club meetings. He helped start five new churches in the area.

As I reflected on Elias' journey, I began to understand why God took him from success to poverty. The church in Chiapas was the wilderness for Elias, where God prepared and shaped him for the work in Oaxaca. Elias learned to be even more compassionate through experiencing poverty on his own. Those trying years were the fire that burned away all that is unnecessary, and brought forth a man with a pure and sincere heart. By the time Elias came to direct the outreach in Oaxaca, he had learned to hear God speaking and to follow what God said.

Elias could have stayed in Mexico City and lived what many might think is a successful life, but he would have missed so much. He is now affecting many more lives because he listened to that still, small voice within. He now enjoys the blessings that come from being tried and found true.

Dedication

Don't urge me to leave you or to turn back from you...May the Lord deal with me, be it ever so severely, if anything but death separates you and me.
Ruth 1:16,17

Elias would enjoy the help of another person in Oaxaca who came to us at a special time. In Mexico, a doctor must perform two years of social medicine, serving in a government clinic or a non-profit organization, after completing medical school. Antonio requested that the government allow doctors to complete their two years of social medicine in the clinic. The government granted the request and sent a young doctor by the name of Maria de la Luz.

When Maria first arrived, her feelings were typical of most graduate doctors. She wanted to hurry through her two years' requirement so she could get into private practice. However, as she worked for the clinic, new feelings awakened within her. "Each day I saw the poor people coming to me for help because they had nothing," she explained. "Yet they would offer a chicken or something else when it may have been the only thing they had. They seemed so appreciative of what I did for them." Each trip to Oaxaca, I saw Dr. Maria changing, or rather blossoming. She showed more and more compassion on the people, and her walk with God grew stronger every day.

When Dr. Maria had completed her term, she hesitated as she pondered what to do with her future. At one time, her great desire was to go into private practice, but something had happened during the two years with "Manos de Ayuda." She told Antonio that she wanted to continue working in the clinic. Antonio said, "You know we cannot pay you what you could obtain if you went into practice."

Maria paused for a moment and said, "I know you cannot pay me much but I cannot leave these people."

Her salary at the clinic began at $350 per month. This was

extremely low, especially considering what doctors in the United States make. Yet, Maria continued to work at the clinic, showering her patients with her beautiful smiles, as if she were completely content, which I believe she was. She looked like she loved her job, and felt secure in doing it.

The love and compassion she showed to the poorest of the poor would continue for years with Manos de Ayuda. Eventually, she became the medical director. What a joy to observe her as she listened carefully to an elderly Indian tell her health problem, or

The author and Antonio Vazquez with a boy from the dump who had received surgery on his leg. He can now walk normally. Antonio directed the work for 13 years before having to retire, due to heart problems. Photo, NWMT.

put her arms around a person and express her love. She was a special help to our teams as well, by screening patients for them. Her smile and her desire to help caused our teams to love Dr. Maria. Her name is so fitting. Translated, it means Maria of the light. She has certainly been a shining light to her people and a light for God.

After nine years with Manos de Ayuda, Maria faced another life-changing decision. After working closely with our surgical teams for a long time, one of our surgeons talked with Dr. Maria and suggested she go back to school to specialize in ophthalmology. Maria agreed and was admitted into a university in Mexico.

Though we hated to see her go, we all understood that it was an incredible opportunity for her. She had given many years of service to her people. Now she could pursue something she loved. This would also provide her with more income since few ophthalmologists existed in Oaxaca.

She carefully prepared for her departure. At the last moment, she walked into Elias and said, "I cannot do it!"

Elias was surprised, and asked, "Why?"

Dr. Maria said, "I believe God wants me to stay. I feel I can be more helpful to our people doing what I am doing." Within a few days, she turned down the school. She stayed as the medical director for Manos de Ayuda.

Many people might consider her decision to be foolish. She was throwing away a wonderful opportunity. She had already given so much to her people that she should think a little of herself, too. Yet, God has a plan for all of us, and no matter what others say, we are mistaken to ever stray from the path He has laid for us. The Bible reminds us that God's ways are not our ways. Though appearances may be deceiving, and everyone may say the choice is foolish, it is always wise to follow the guidance God gives.

I know how Dr. Maria must have wrestled with that issue. After years of directing NWMT, I was offered an opportunity to earn a high six-figure salary. I was excited about the offer. I said to Jean, "This could be our opportunity to secure our retirement. I feel that it would be all right to take this job, because I have spent many years in service." I added, "I'm in my fifties, and it makes sense to spend some time earning enough for us to enjoy our later years."

We agreed to pray about it, first. After a period of time, I asked Jean, "How do you feel about my leaving to take the position?"

Jean answered, "I do not feel good about you doing this."

Her answer did not surprise me, because I felt the same way. I felt very secure when I contacted the person who offered me the position. I said, "If God has not released me from this work, you would not want me, for I would fail."

Thus, I understood Dr. Maria's decision. She had not been released to go to a specialty school. It's a decision she has never questioned. Her life has purpose because she is participating in what she is called to do, and this brings her a deep happiness. Also, when wrestling with a major decision like that, and then making the right choice, there is a security in the work like never before. Perhaps God brings conflicts like that into our lives to confirm that we are doing what is meant for us to do. Perhaps it is His way of renewing our sense of purpose. As for me, I have learned it is better to earn a five-figure salary than to be in the wrong place.

Dr. Maria and Elias showed their commitment to the mission in many ways. For example, they both decided to learn English, so they could communicate better with our teams. For two years, they attended school five nights a week after putting in full days. Now, they both speak English very well. What dedication they have shown to their calling!

In 1998, I was talking to Antonio on the phone. Something did not seem right. I asked, "Are you feeling all right?"

"No," he replied.

"What is wrong?" I questioned.

"I am experiencing shortness of breath and I have pain in my chest," he answered.

"Please go to your doctor right away," I said.

"Yes, I will do that," Antonio said. The doctor examined him and gave specific requirements for rest. He told Antonio to leave his position or risk serious heart problems. Neither of us wanted to hear that, yet neither of us wanted him to risk his health either. At the age of sixty, Antonio resigned as the director of Manos de Ayuda.

Antonio had put in twelve hard working years. The man was inspiring because he worked so hard. He made things look easy to outsiders, but to those who know the effort needed to succeed, we were amazed at what he could accomplish. Antonio is a faithful servant who showed his dedication to his God by being dedicated to his people. Thousands benefited from Antonio's life work. He continues to participate in the mission as an elder statesman for the mission in Mexico. The Lord will have a special reward for this brother.

Elias took over Antonio's position. As Elijah carefully trained Elisha as a prophet of the Lord, Antonio trained Elias to perform the duties as director of the Mexico outreach. Both men are great leaders, and the passing of the mantle was a smooth transition.

In assuming the role of director of all the work in Mexico, Elias would need a leader for the work in Oaxaca. The Lord provided another simple changing of the guards as Elias gave the position to Dr. Maria de la Luz.

Antonio, Elias, and Dr. Maria all could have been extremely successful in the secular world. Yet, all of them gave up their chance to be successful in the eyes of others, and instead became servants of others. They discovered what it truly means to put "others before self." Jesus said, "I have come to serve not to be served." He also said, "If you love me feed my children." Though they will never be rich in this world, they are rich in the kingdom of God, for it is there that they have placed their heart and their treasure. God does not care about earthly wealth. He will not allow us to take it when we die. The only gifts that God will accept are the deeds we have done for others.

I have often thought about that night when I got up from my easy chair. It was the best move I ever made. The experiences of God's wonderful love has been shown to me through people like Dr. Maria, Elias, Antonio and hundreds more. These people share the same priority, "Love the Lord your God with all your heart, with all your soul and with all your mind, and love your neighbor as yourself." What a different world this would be if more of us followed this commandment!

CHAPTER EIGHT

THE POWER OF TOUCH

A man with leprosy came and knelt before him and said, "Lord, if you are
willing, you can make me clean." Jesus reached out his hand and touched
the man. "I am willing," he said. "Be clean!" Matthew 8:2,3

"I knew if I showed her my report card without straight A's,
I would be punished," explained a 17-year-old boy who described
in court how he killed his mother with an ax. Undergoing extreme
punishments since he was four years old, the boy said that his
mother physically and verbally abused him. He added that she
never spoke words of love or ever touched him. Finally, to avoid
her wrath again, he picked up an ax and killed her.

Such a story is not altogether uncommon to read. In our
fast-paced culture and its demand for excellence, an element that
is vitally important for our children is often missing. Perhaps we
underestimate the power of a pat on the back, a squeeze of the
hand, a kiss on the cheek, or an old-fashioned bear hug.

Once Jesus was speaking to a crowd, and a group of children came to him. His disciples were annoyed and urged them to
leave. I can understand what the disciples were feeling. When
our children were young and we were entertaining, sometimes the
children's play became so disruptive that I found myself irritated
and would ask them to play elsewhere.

The children around Jesus were probably playing and
being a little too loud. The disciples were concerned that the exu-
berance of the children might interfere with Jesus' message to the
crowd. Jesus rebuffed the disciples by saying, "Do not stop these
children from approaching me." He added that we should be like
these children in our relationship with the Heavenly Father. Then

Jesus did something very important. The scripture tells us that he touched the children and departed.

I can see His actions clearly in my mind. He looks straight into each child's eyes, bending down so as to be on an equal level. He hugs one rambunctious child, pats an older boy on the shoulder, lightly touches the cheek of a shy girl and smiles. Jesus did that because God created us to be loved and touched. He understood that without touching, we would not develop into the person God wants us to be.

This truth was brought to my attention in 1990, when we were shocked by the television images of naked children in the run-down orphanages of Romania. It was difficult to believe that children were treated in the way the news had described. Approximately 200,000 children were being warehoused in state-run institutions under deplorable conditions.

The communist dictator, Nicolai Ceaucescu, had decreed that women should have five children, and families were penalized for not obeying the mandate. His goal was to build up a special army in hopes of attaining worldwide power much the same as Hitler tried to do by raising the Hitler youth.

However, the economy of Romania was in shambles and families could not afford five children. The average worker made about $25 a month. This would not even put enough food on the table. Reluctantly, parents had to turn children over to the state-run institutions.

The state workers graded the children as to which institution they would be sent. If a child had no physical or mental blemish, they were sent to an institution that raised them in the communist doctrine. If a child had any physical or mental condition, including minor deformities such as a cleft lip, club feet, or even strabismus (crossed eyes), they were sent to what was referred to as the Institute For Irrecoverables. A child with a slight disability was often grouped with a child who had a severe mental illness.

Within the orphanages, the conditions were terrible. Newborn babies and small children were often placed in unheated buildings where temperatures would reach below freezing.

Their diets were meager, and the children slowly starved. They were given no clothes, and would often lay in their waste for days. When they cried, they were beaten. Forty percent of the children died each year, though almost all of them had correctable problems.

The orphans in all of the institutions were rarely touched by the staff. They were never picked up and held, nor were they allowed to play or have objects on which to focus their attention. As a result, the orphans developed many physical and mental problems. Children would sit in their cribs, rocking back and forth, continuously. Some would beat their heads against the cribs.

Scientists from all over the world began studying the Romanian orphans. Many important questions about child development were answered, and these discoveries helped parents and caregivers of children around the world.

Using imagery, scientists compared the brains of normal children with those of Romanian orphans, and discovered vast differences. A spider web has many single strands of web that all

The author with a Romanian Orphan. These orphans were warehoused for years in unbelievable conditions, thousands dying every year or becoming problem children from lack of care. Photo, NWMT.

connect with each other to form a pattern. Similarly, a normal child's brain will have "connectors" that cover the brain. However, in a Romanian orphan's brain, these strands do not connect.

Scientists concluded that these connectors need to form during the first two years of life in order to develop sensory perception. If they do not connect, the child will develop severe learning disabilities, have slow growth, develop abnormal behaviors, lack of trust, and lack of love. They will have moderate to severe emotional problems, and will crave attention. Many of the girls and boys upon leaving the orphanages turn to prostitution both for the money and for the human contact they never had.

The orphans were also developing problems due to severe nutritional deficiencies. The state provided about fifty cents a day to feed the children in the better orphanages. Yet, this was not enough to provide any kind of nutritional balance and the children developed health and mental problems.

The children's environment was badly in need of improvement. The buildings of the orphanages were deteriorating. During the winter, snow often blew into the children's rooms through broken windows. Showers, toilets, and sinks did not work. Children's mattresses were ripped and stained with urine. Important appliances such as laundry machines were often missing.

Pure Religion
Religion that God our Father accepts as pure and faultless is this: to look after orphans and widows in their distress and to keep oneself from being polluted by the world. James 1:27

When the news of the condition of the orphans reached our televisions, the board decided to begin an outreach to the orphans of Romania. Through prayer, we searched for a way to make a difference in the orphans' lives.

The dictator Ceaucescu was overthrown in 1989. The new Romanian government started allowing people from around the world to adopt certain children. However, orphans from the Institute For Irrecoverables were not allowed to be adopted.

Babies with crossed eyes, club feet, cleft lips and other easily correctable birth defects, did not have a chance to live a normal life with a family.

Thus, the orphans who could not be adopted became our first area of concern. By recruiting specialty medical teams to perform corrective surgeries, perhaps we could eliminate any excuse to keep a child in the Institute For Irrecoverables. The state would move the children out of the Institute For Irrecoverables into a normal institution, which would give them a better chance for adoption.

We sent Doug Rawlins to assess the situation in the institutions. Doug first discovered a lack of basic medical equipment in Romania. Much of the equipment they owned was thirty to forty years old. We found they lacked many of the tools our own hospitals take for granted. In order to perform surgeries, all the equipment would have to be gathered in the United States and then sent to Romania.

Once again, God provided the transportation as before. Donna Nelson, the senior vice-president of Evergreen Airlines in McMinnville, Oregon, was moved by the plight of the orphans and believed her company could help us. She went on our behalf to the owner and president, Del Smith. Del agreed to donate the use of one of the 727 airplanes to fly medical equipment, supplies, and our first surgical team to Romania.

Doug flew ahead of the team to prepare for the team's arrival. He enlisted the help of a Romanian orthopedic surgeon by the name of Radu Radulescu. In the meantime, we recruited our first surgical team for Romania, an ophthalmology team led by Dr. Royce Fonken.

Evergreen Airlines flew their plane into the Portland Airport where we loaded it with all the necessary items. It was an exciting day when the team departed. All of the Portland television stations were present for the take-off.

Doug planned to meet the team members when they arrived in Romania. Later, Doug related an interesting story of being on the Bucharest, Romania airport tarmac with Dr. Radu, awaiting the arrival of our first surgical team:

"The plane had been delayed when it had stopped for fuel in Newfoundland. Unfortunately I had no way of knowing that. Dr. Radu and I had been waiting out in the freezing cold for three hours. Finally, I turned to Radu and told him he need not wait any longer, but that I would continue waiting. When I had said this, Radu said, "Are you kidding? We have been waiting forty-five years for the Americans to arrive. What's a few more hours?" Tears filled my eyes as I realized how long these people had been under the bondage of Communism. I was glad we were coming to help them in their time of need."

Dr. Radulescu became the director for our work in Romania. He screened children from the orphanages to ensure they were ready for surgery when the teams arrived. Eventually, Radu was able to come to America for special training on arthroscopic surgery. This method allows the surgeon to use a small incision to insert a tube that has a camera on one end. Then, the surgeon can view the problem area on a television screen and perform a less invasive surgery. He became the first Romanian surgeon to use this method in his own country. He also trained many other surgeons in the use of the arthroscopic equipment provided.

Our hopes bloomed into reality when some of the first children who were operated on by the initial team were adopted right away by families from the United States. Our medical teams performed many different types of corrective surgeries and freed many orphans from the Institution for Irrecoverables. NWMT became the number one agency in the world doing the most surgeries for the orphans of Romania.

For the orphans who would never be adopted, our goal was to improve their environment. They were living in distressingly archaic and run-down buildings. Many improvements were made by sending non-medical teams to make repairs to the buildings. Just as the non-medical groups had gone to help with projects in Mexico, hundreds of teams went and continue to go to Romania repairing one orphanage after another. Volunteers have replaced broken windows to keep the snow out in the winter. They also repaired showers, toilets, sinks and faucets, as well as replaced the urine-stained mattresses, installed heating systems and laundry equipment, built playgrounds and accomplished many other improvements.

During the many visits to Romania, I observed church or civic groups work to improve the condition of an orphanage. Made up of people from a variety of backgrounds and skills, these teams are willing to do the "grunt" work. Some unskilled women and men took a few lessons before arriving in Romania and became window replacement professionals by practicing on the

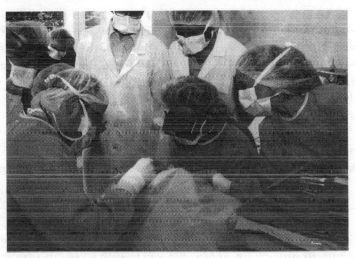

NWMT eye surgery team performing surgery on a child in Moldova.
NWMT is refurbishing this hospital which sees more than ten-thousand
children per year. Photo NWMT.

orphanages. Untrained would-be plumbers tinkered under the cabinets of many appliances, attaining an expert status of quick-fixes by the end of their trip. Their desire to help the orphans drove them to attempt tasks which they knew nothing about before.

These teams showed their love in ways other than hard work. People would break down and weep over the plight of the orphans. During the short time they were in Romania, they would quickly build relationships with the orphans. Often, parting times were spent in tears. Many returned to Romania again to do more because they saw the difference they made.

The physical environment was not our only concern. A program to train Romanian orphanage staff in infant stimulation, a method which helps infants' brains to develop normally, began. Many teams of infant stimulation specialists have been to Romania since to teach the method. Sadly, this program will take years to reach most of the orphanages. Old ways do not change over night. Patience is needed. It is enough to celebrate each child who develops normally.

As we became more involved with the orphanages, we learned that children were released from the institutions once they turned eighteen years old. They were sent out without any training or other skills that would enable them to obtain a job, or survive on their own. Many children turned to prostitution and others to street crime.

The solution for this problem was to give them Jesus Christ. He was the only One who could be with them always, and would not fail. Few of these children knew anything about God, and little knowledge was available.

We asked the directors of the institutions if we could begin a weekly children's Bible club program. To our surprise, they granted our request. Because we had been starting Bible club programs in Mexico for years, we were able to begin programs in Romania quickly and easily. Our new orphanage clubs consisted of children meeting with a Romanian Christian once a week, where they were taught songs and scripture. The leader read a Bible story, explained it, and attempted to make it applicable to the children's daily routine. The Bible clubs eventually reached thirteen orphanages with an average attendance rate of 1,500 orphans.

Probably the most outstanding lesson our medical and non-medical teams learned while working with the Romanian orphans, was the importance of touching. Each person quickly saw the tremendous response they received by holding, touching and loving these children. The children often clung to volunteers in groups of five or six. They craved a loving, caring set of hands to hold them. Many a volunteer would weep as they prepared to leave on their last day, having established a special bond with several children.

The plight of the Romanian orphans should be a constant reminder of the importance of touch and encouragement. As parents and grandparents, we can learn from the tragedies of untouched children, and remember to hug and hold a little more, and demand a little less. If we respond thus, then the sufferings of the orphans of Romania will not have been completely in vain.

Though conditions have improved some, the orphanages in Romania are still crowded with orphans. The need for repair teams and baby stimulation training still exists.

CHAPTER NINE

PERMISSION TO PLUNDER

The spoils belong to Allah and the Apostle. Koran, Chapter 8

The door burst open and armed men rushed into her house screaming orders to her father and brother to move out. Frightened, nine year old Paymon grabbed her mother's hand as they were shoved out into the street. Her father and brother were herded down the road along with many other men and boys, who had also been forced out of their homes by soldiers.

Soon, they reached the outskirts of the village. The soldiers pushed them towards a field. When they reached the field, the soldiers shouted more orders. Paymon stood beside her mother, gripping tightly to her mother's hand, shaking and crying with fear. "Mommy, why are they making all the men dig the hole?" she asked. She knew something bad was happening but she did not understand. Her mother gripped her hand tightly and patted her on the head with her other hand.

The men and boys completed the big hole in the ground. A man screamed for them to line up next to the trench. The little girl began to sob. She cried, "Don't hurt my Papa!" The cry would never leave her heart. The soldiers took aim and fired into the group of men and boys. Her father and brother spun around as the bullets ripped through their bodies. A bulldozer pushed dirt over the still warm bodies of all the men and boys of her village. The little girl would never forget this day. It had been seared into her memory forever. Hundreds of stories like this would be repeated.

* * * * *

In 1988, a television personality announced on Iraqi television that a great day had come, a gift from Allah. "God is great!" said the announcer, "God has given us permission to plunder the treacherous Kurds." The events that followed this momentous announcement were terrible. Saddam Hussein's army and secret police unleashed a savage and unrestrained war on the Kurdish people. They plundered homes, raped women, shot the males, burned their crops and even gassed whole villages. Nearly 4,000 villages were destroyed in the quest to annihilate the thorn in Saddam Hussein's side, the Kurdish population in Northern Iraq.

The term, "permission to plunder," is from the eighth chapter of the Koran which is titled "Al-Anfal" (The Spoils). When a leader like Saddam Hussein declares "permission to plunder," he is giving his people license to plunder, loot, rape, and massacre. He uses the term for the destruction of the Christians, Jews, or even Muslims in the case of the Kurds.

Just as the Bible has been misinterpreted to excuse hateful actions, so also the Koran. Most Muslims who have studied the Koran do not believe the meaning of the scripture is to eliminate another group of people. However, leaders such as Saddam Hussein or Hitler will use religion to accomplish their purposes. Evil people have always used the name of God to achieve their goals. God must be both angered and grieved when His name is used for wickedness.

The Kurds are not Arab, though the predominant religion is Islam. They relate more to Europeans than to Arabs. At one time, Kurdistan was its own independent nation which covered an area that presently is part of Iraq, Turkey, Syria, Iran and even Russia. After World War I, Britain divided the area for political reasons. The Kurds are now the largest group in the world without a country, numbering more than 22 million people.

The Kurds have always been a proud and productive people, working the prosperous land of Northern Iraq. Throughout the rolling hills and small mountains, they grow wheat, apples and raise large herds of cattle, goats and sheep. Intent on destroying the economy and lives of the Kurds, Saddam burned the Kurds' wheat and apple orchards, and killed or carried off most of their herd animals. From 1988 until 1991, Saddam's army attacked the defenseless Kurds, killing at will, and forcing many men to join his army so he could use them to kill their neighbors.

Following the Gulf War of 1991, the Kurds in Northern Iraq were encouraged to rebel against Saddam. The Kurdish Rebel Army drove Saddam's forces out in hopes of an autonomous state. However, Saddam regrouped his forces and came back with a renewed vengeance. He sent the Republican Army with tanks and artillery, and their brutal methods caused the Kurds to flee with only the clothes on their backs. They fled into the freezing mountains along the Turkish border. However, because Turkey had been at war with the Kurdish Rebels for many years, they would not permit the Kurdish civilians to cross over into Turkey for protection.

The extreme weather of the high, snow-packed mountains began to take its toll. Nearly every family lost children and aged ones to exposure and hunger. Babies were buried by the hundreds. It seemed as if even nature was attempting to annihilate the Kurds.

Help finally came through the United Nations. The same coalition forces who fought the Gulf War against Saddam started dropping food, medicine, and tents to the Kurdish in the mountains. President Bush told the Iraqi Army to pull back or be attacked. He also sent in forces to assure that the Iraqi army retreated.

The United Nation's forces attempted to communicate to the Kurds, telling them to come down from the mountains where food, shelter, and medical care awaited them. Our forces did a magnificent job of constructing a city of camps almost overnight. It was one of the greatest efforts ever undertaken in modern times to save such a large group of people.

The Kurdish people were so frightened that it took days to convince them they would be safe from Saddam. At first, they trickled slowly into the camps, and then they came in droves. Thousands of cold, sick, and hungry people staggered to safety. As we watched these scenes on television news, I knew that it was time for Northwest Medical Teams to reach out to the Kurds.

Restoring Hope

...but we also rejoice in our sufferings, because we know that suffering produces perseverance; perseverance, character; and character, hope. And hope does not disappoint us, because God has poured out his love into our hearts by the Holy Spirit, whom he has given us. Romans 5:3-5

The two huge blades of the German Army transport helicopter turned slowly. Picking up speed, the blades caused the helicopter to vibrate. It lifted straight up 1000 feet and hovered for several minutes. Then, it moved forward, picking up speed. We continued to fly low, and I wondered why. My neighbor leaned over and said, "Look out the window!"

I gazed through one of the small windows. Below us, a United States' Army helicopter gun ship flew only a hundred feet to our side. Someone seated on the opposite side said, "There is one off the other side also!"

All the doors on both sides of the gunships were open, and in each doorway a soldier stood ready to operate a very large machine gun. Now, I understood. We were flying low with two escorts to protect us from ground fire.

I was traveling with a group of television and newspaper reporters to join the two medical teams in Zakhu, Iraq. Helicopters were the only way to get into the area where the medical teams were working with the Kurds.

The Kurds had many needs. One of them was met by another agency, International Rescue Committee, who built camps and latrines for the people. Northwest Medical Teams faced the immense challenge of saving severely malnourished and dehydrated children and babies.

Our two teams divided up to reach as many suffering people as possible. One team ran a clinic in the middle of a huge tent city set up by United States' military forces in a wheat field just outside Zakhu. The other team flew by helicopter to the mountains where thousands had stayed, fearing Saddam Hussein's army. As I flew into the mountains to visit our team, I could see the hundreds of tents. The Kurds were camping along streams and valleys. The military was bringing clean drinking water and food to them by helicopter, while setting up a filter to obtain clean water from the contaminated streams. It was sad to see these proud people living in such conditions.

When I arrived, I met with a British Army colonel who was in charge of the area. He showed me where our team was working. As we were talking, the ground suddenly shook from a very large explosion. I almost dove to the ground, but I noticed the British officer had not flinched. "What was that?" I asked.

"Oh, sorry about that!" he calmly explained. "We just exploded more land mines. Saddam's army has set land mines throughout the mountain area. Each day, we explode the mines we find in a hole." Sadly, Saddam's mines would continue to blow Kurds apart for years to come.

Our team was accomplishing many difficult tasks behind the military lines. They were examining many patients. Cholera, which is caused from drinking contaminated water, was a main concern. The sickness must be treated quickly since it can kill within twenty-four hours; thus, a separate tent for cholera patients was set up.

One day, United Nations' representatives gathered all the international agencies to discuss problems in a nearby city, Dohuk, which was approximately thirty miles away. Many people were suffering and needed help. Iraqi troops were lined up in front of the city, and in order to meet the needs, they must pass through hostile territory.

United Nations' officials planned for a military convoy to travel to Dohuk the next day, bringing supplies and volunteers to aid those living there. The mission was risky. All the members of other agencies declined. However, Dr. Travis Cavens decided to lead members of our team to offer medical assistance. When I discovered they had gone, I was filled with mixed emotions, wavering between concern for their safety, and pride for their courage.

United Nations' military forces accompanied the team into Dohuk without incident. Immediately, the team began screening the sick and meeting the most urgent needs. They continued to work with the people for several days.

One evening, agents of the Iraqi secret police slipped into the area and began firing their weapons. Inside the hotel, our team was frightened to hear bullets hitting the outside walls. Since UN police had assured the team protection, Dr. Cavens watched the shooting for awhile, waiting for UN police to intervene. When the firing continued, he hastily retreated with the team into the basement of the hotel for safety, only to find the UN police hiding there as well! When Dr. Cavens discovered they were working without real protection, he was forced to return with the team to Zakhu.

In return for safety and help, the Kurds rewarded the U.S. military and medical teams with affection. Whenever we passed by, they would stop and wave. Men would salute us. Children learned to say "hello, mister," to male and female alike. They reminded us often that they were thankful for our presence, in spite of our religious and cultural differences. Though they were predominately Muslim, no aid had come from any Muslim country; all help had come from the Christian West.

In June of 1991, the Kurds heard that military forces would be leaving. Panicking, they readied themselves to flee to the mountains once again. UN officials convinced them to stay, explaining that some military personnel would remain, and jet fighters would fly over the area daily to warn the Iraqi Army not to cross the line. The Kurds were comforted. They anticipated seeing the jet fighters go overhead, which was a sign of safety for them.

As the U.S. military began to pull its forces out of Northern Iraq, it requested that NWMT take over the large medical warehouse to distribute millions of dollars in medicine and medical supplies to the other private volunteer agencies. We agreed, but did not realize what a lengthy task we had undertaken. Over a year later, we were still running the warehouse, distributing 90 percent of all medical relief supplies used by the agencies during the relief effort. Over the length of our time in Northern Iraq, NWMT distributed over $30 million dollars in medical supplies.

After the immediate needs of the Kurdish people were met, the medical teams returned home. However, we could not pull out completely because we had made the commitment to the military to oversee the distribution of medical supplies. We prayed for a director to coordinate this part of our ministry. God already was working on an answer to meet our request in an unusual way.

Good Trees

By their fruit you will recognize them. Do people pick grapes from thorn-bushes, or figs from thistles? Likewise, every good tree bears good fruit...
Matthew 7:16-17

"I am not sure what we can do, but let's do something!" said Mike Carson to his wife, Mary and his friend, Bob Blincoe. Soon, the group, along with Bob's wife and children, was flying from Amman, Jordan to Ankara, Turkey where they would catch a military helicopter into Zakhu, Iraq.

Their spontaneous decision paid off. When the United Nations' military entered Northern Iraq, they brought plenty of supplies: tents, blankets, forklifts, food, water, and medicine. However, once they arrived, officials discovered they had over-looked an essential part to their mission — translators. Mike and Bob entered the scene like Arabic-speaking angels sent from heaven. With a sigh of relief, officials assigned the group to the refugee camp to run the registration of the Kurds. As they worked, they also learned Kurdish.

All the members of the Carson and Blincoe families were called to be workers to the Kurdish people. They had gone to Jordan to study language with the hopes the Iraqi government would allow them to enter Northern Iraq to work among the Kurds. These families did not want to reach the Kurds through preaching. Instead, they wished to live among them, while per-forming good works. They wanted to preach Christ by example, rather than words.

The Carson and Blincoe families knew their calling, but God hadn't provided instructions on how to accomplish that call-ing. Similarly, NWMT was given the use of a huge warehouse for medical supplies, but God had not provided the director, yet. These missing puzzle pieces were about to come together for a perfect fit.

While on a trip to Zukhu, Stu Wilcuts, who was organizing NWMT programs, met Bob Blincoe. When Bob shared his goals, Stu immediately knew that he was the one for whom we had been praying. He asked Bob to help. Bob discussed the proposition with Mike, and they both volunteered. After I met the duo, I agreed that the two men would be qualified. Bob became the volunteer director and Mike became the assistant volunteer director.

Bob moved his family to Zakhu; Mike and Mary moved to Dohuk, south of Zakhu, where Mary gave birth to their first child, a son named Jason. These families were the only American families living in Northern Iraq at the time.

Bob and Mike showed tremendous insight in setting up a program that properly distributed medicines and supplies to other humanitarian agencies and to Kurdish hospitals. Mike developed a computer system, with the help of a USAID contract, to link Kurdish hospitals together. This helped hospital employees to know which health problems existed in different parts of the country, and where medicines were located.

Bob handled one of his first projects with a little humor. In the 1980's, Saddam Hussein's army confiscated all of the donkeys which the mountain people used for travel and carrying supplies. This action cut off any incoming supplies for the winter, because they had no access to the main road.

In response, Bob began "Project Hee-Haw," using the slogan, "MULES 'R' US." In one of his newsletters, he wrote, "When you need a thousand donkeys, and you gotta have 'em fast, who ya gonna call?" The answer was the United States Office of Foreign Disaster Assistance (OFDA) who donated over 1000 donkeys to deliver to remote mountain communities. Bob and Kurdish workers chose villages on the basis of need and delivered 1010 donkeys. Bob said, "In every village community, it was an event which will always be remembered gratefully."

The dedication of the Blincoe and Carson families is admirable. Enduring many difficulties as they lived and worked in Northern Iraq, they continued to perform good deeds. Their fruits not only drew the Kurds to them, they also attracted many enemies. The Iraqi Secret Police eventually put a reward on Bob and Mike's lives because they hated the good works they were doing for the Kurds. In fact, for security reasons I have changed a few names. The Kurdish Rebel Army guarded the families day and night. Still, Bob's house was burglarized and death threats were written on his living room wall. The threats did not deter the families. All of them believed they were where God could use them.

Bob was asked to teach a United States' history class at the Dohuk University. He agreed to teach if he was given the freedom to tell all of our history, including the Christian foundation of our country. Surprisingly, they agreed. The aid workers had laid a groundwork of love and care for the Kurdish people, and perhaps this is why Bob was allowed certain privileges.

The love for the Kurdish people did not go unnoticed. When I traveled with Bob, people often yelled greetings to him as we passed. When we were downtown, people approached us and hugged Bob. It was wonderful watching Bob love these people. After history classes, students sometimes visited him to inquire about Christianity. Some came to Mike Carsons house to ask questions about Christianity.

St. Francis of Assisi said, "Preach Christ always and when necessary use words." Bob and Mike served the people the way Christ served, by example. They reflected the real love of Christ. It was a joy to see the genuine love these families had for our Kurdish brothers and sisters.

God and Wrigley's Chewing Gum

I tell you the truth, if you have faith as small as a mustard seed, you can say to this mountain, 'Move from here to there' and it will move. Nothing will be impossible for you. Matthew 17:20,21

We left in Bob's utility van. We passed Dohuk, the Kurdish rebel army's last outpost, and within two miles, we arrived at the first Iraqi army checkpoint. My heart beat fast. A lump formed in my throat. We were Americans in hostile territory. The American army had just defeated them. How would they respond to us, their enemy?

As we approached the checkpoint, I looked across the rolling hills of wheat. On every knoll, as far as the eye could see, a tank sat with its gun pointed north to the Kurdish. They seemed ready to attack in force at any time. Silently, I prayed, "Lord, I ask for your protection." Inwardly, I questioned, "Had we made the right decision?" We were penetrating Iraqi military lines in an attempt to help the Kurds, whom Iraqis hated. This was no small adventure.

* * * * *

In 1992, many private volunteer agencies were planning to pull out of Iraq because of lack of funds. I traveled to Dohuk with the intention of also closing our operations. However, after arriving, the needs were still apparent and urgent. People were in tents without heat and with only a few blankets. Bob and I knew many would get sick during the winter months.

Rather than shutting down, I promised Jim and the Kurdish workers that I would return to ask donors to continue the medical programs. Even then, I could not foresee that NWMT would end up with as many as 150 Kurdish workers, continuing to help in that part of the world for six years.

Our donors responded to the need. In April of 1992, I returned to Iraq. Living conditions had improved, but a new threat hovered over the people like an ominous storm cloud.

Before they were attacked, all of the Kurdish veterinarians had worked for the government. When the government fled from Northern Iraq, it left the Kurdish without any veterinary program. The veterinarians were broke; thus, no veterinary services had been performed for over a year.

Livestock was an important element to the Kurdish livelihood. Because their economy had collapsed, herd animals were as important as money. Without medicines to vaccinate and heal the cattle, goats, and sheep, many would die. The failure of the livestock would have terrible consequences.

The lack of animal vaccinations was the most immediate

need. The cattle contracted hoof and mouth, cattle fever, and other diseases. The sheep were infected with parasites. Unless the animals were given medicine and vaccine soon, the whole live-stock population was at risk of perishing.

Bob sought help from the United Nations and the United States State Department, but he feared that by the time they acted, the animals would die. He asked if Northwest Medical Teams, which was the largest agency working in Northern Iraq, could help while he continued to seek assistance elsewhere.

Though Bob had purchased vaccine from Europe, it would take valuable time to reach us. The animals needed vaccinations immediately. Bob discovered that vaccine was available in a city near to us called Mosul. A Kurdish worker knew a Kurdish man in Mosul who had access to vaccine. Ironically, he could obtain it from the Iraqi government without them knowing where it was going. The Kurdish man said he would be willing to risk his own life to obtain the vaccine to help save the animals. Mosul was located just forty miles away, but the miles were behind the Iraqi Army lines. Bob said he was going to penetrate the military lines, pick up the vaccinations after dark, and bring them back.

Saddam had placed an in country embargo on anything going north to the Kurdish. All vehicles were searched, and anything that could benefit the Kurdish was confiscated. Military officials often pulled cars over to the side of the road to drain the diesel, allowing the vehicle only enough to reach their destination. The extra diesel was burned on the side of the road. They would never consider allowing vaccines to reach the Kurdish.

* * * * *

Bob said, "We'll have to pass through three or four check-points each way.

I asked, Bob, isn't that a bit dangerous?"

"Yes, it is. However, I am going to tell them I am with the United Nations. If this Kurdish man is willing to risk his life, surely I can try to help." He added, "This Kurdish man in Mosul would be executed if he was caught."

It was this kind of love demonstrated many times by Bob and Mike that would endear them to the Kurdish people. I asked Bob, "Who are you taking with you?"

He answered, "I will not allow anyone to accompany me."

I could not let that happen. I said, "I'm going with you."

Bob reminded me, "Ron, I have papers that allow me to be here legally. You entered through the back door of Turkey and have no visa to be in Iraq."

The reason the others and I had to enter through Turkey was because the Iraqi government would not grant visas to aid workers. Bob had obtained his before the war. Yet, I still could not let Bob go alone. I would suffer far more if something happened to Bob and I was not there to help. After I insisted, Jim said, "Okay."

We approached the first checkpoint and my stomach tightened. We were motioned to stop by a military policeman. The soldier asked us, "Who are you?"

Bob explained, "We are Americans on our way to Mosul. We are working with the United Nations and we need supplies." When the young soldier heard him say "Americans," a smile came over his face. After listening to Bob's explanation, he waved us through.

Later, the soldier returned to my mind. His smiling face reminded me that people are not our enemies. Instead we fight against corrupt governments, dictators, and generals. After years of traveling to places like Russia and other former communist countries whose people I once believed were my enemies, I discovered they were people just like me. They loved their families and only wanted to work and live in peace.

We passed through several other checkpoints before arriving in Mosul in the afternoon. We were waiting until dark to go to the safe house, so we were able to explore Mosul. The ancient city had once been called by another name — Nineveh. Centuries ago, Jonah walked into the city and told the people they had forty days to repent before God destroyed them.

Jonah's journey must have been difficult. After weathering a terrific tempest, waiting three days in the belly of the whale, and then being spit up onto the mainland, Jonah then had to travel more than 150 miles inland, which was a three-days' journey, to preach to the Ninevites.

Bob drove around where the old city had been. Some of the old walls and gates still stood. I imagined the king listening to Jonah's report. He falls to the ground, and tears his clothes in repentance. He declares a fast, and seeks the forgiveness of God. All the people follow his actions (Jonah 3:4-10). During the forty days, the people turn from their evil ways, and wait in hope for their deliverance. Their sorrow ultimately gives way to joy as the people experience God's compassion, mercy and forgiveness. I have felt the warmth of God's grace whenever I have reflected upon God's forgiveness. I know how they felt.

The sun set; soon after, twilight twinkled its purple brilliance over Mosul. When darkness came, we drove to the safe house where the vaccine was stored. As we pulled up, I suggested to Bob, "I'll stay in the van. I do not want to take the chance of the Iraqi secret police making me identify this courageous man. I will look straight ahead while you put the boxes in the van."

When I heard Bob close the back door, I looked behind me. The whole rear of the van was filled to the ceiling with boxes. When Bob climbed into the driver's seat, I asked, "How are we going to pass through the checkpoints with so many boxes? There are windows in the back, and the police will see them at the first checkpoint." I paused, fear seizing my heart. "There's no way we can hide that many boxes," I said.

Bob replied, "I know, but we must try."

A story came to my mind about a man named Brother Andrew. Some called him "God's Smuggler." During the cold war, when it was illegal to own a Bible or for them to be imported into Russia, Brother Andrew would smuggle them into the country. He packed them in suitcases and took them directly through the custom agents. Before passing through customs, he prayed that God would blind the eyes of the agents. Miraculously, he passed the guards without an incident. He smuggled thousands and thousands of Bibles into Russia this way.

I told Bob the story of Brother Andrew. Then, I asked him

to pray with me. "Lord," I prayed aloud, "the Kurdish need this vaccine desperately. Would you blind the eyes of the police at the check points so they will not see what we have? We ask this in the name of Jesus."

When we finished praying, Bob started up the van, and we drove north. We reached the first checkpoint. A guard stood there waving for us to move through. We continued driving with our hearts beating fast, and our mouths whispering thanks to God. At the next checkpoint, the guard waved us through once again.

I saw the lights of Dohuk in the distance, where the Kurdish rebel army waited for our return. The lights were like the lights of home, representing safety and refuge, and these lights were only a mile away. One more checkpoint must be passed to reach it.

Concrete barriers were placed in the roadway to cause vehicles to slow down. This way, no one could speed past the station. Ahead of us, diesel from drained cars burned along the road. Black smoke rose slowly from the road, like a black snake about to strike. The snake image seemed like a bad omen. This check was going to be different.

I felt weak. Various evil scenarios rolled through my mind like previews to horror films. I was in the country illegally, and I was surrounded by guards who were taught to hate my people. I thought of my family and my country that I loved. I have never felt so far away from home.

We stopped. A man stepped out of the guard house. He was not a soldier. He was dressed in civilian clothes, and he looked as if he had not shaved in three days. A hateful expression was on his face. As he approached our vehicle, Bob whispered, "Secret police." I had read and heard of the atrocities committed by the Iraqi Secret Police. I knew they were dangerous.

The man barked out questions in a harsh tone. "Who are you? Where have you been?"

Bob responded quietly. Yet, the man's face did not soften. Instead, it seemed to rage at us, revealing wishes to do us harm. I figured the next question would be, "Where are your papers?" A few days before, two Americans had been thrown into prison for entering the country without papers. If he asked for my papers, prison awaited me.

However, the man did not ask for our papers. Instead, his eyes were suddenly drawn to the contents in the back of our van, which was worse. My heart seemed to fall. I thought, "He sees the boxes!"

The man turned towards the back of the van. Quickly, Bob grabbed a package of Wrigley's chewing gum from the dash. It was such a fast motion that it startled me. He thrust the package of gum out the window, stopping the man in his turn.

"D'you like gum?" Bob asked. The man looked at the gum in Bob's hand and looked at the back several times. Seconds dragged slowly by.

Obviously, the man was wrestling with a decision. It seemed as if he would continue to the back of the van, but then, he turned and grabbed the gum out of Bob's hand. In a gruff voice he said, "Get out of here!"

We drove on, as my heart pounded. "How did you know to reach for the gum, and how did you do it so quickly?" I asked.

Bob answered, "I don't know. My hand grabbed it without my even thinking about it."

We reached Dohuk with the vaccine. Bob hired Kurdish veterinarians and assistants to vaccinate thousands of animals. This action caused the United States Agency for International Development (USAID) to realize the magnitude of the problem. It provided a large grant for us to buy large quantities of vaccines and hire more workers for the program. Soon, Bob's veterinarians were vaccinating 20,000 animals a day. Bob devised a very efficient method for vaccinations, squeezing each dollar. USAID told us that normal overhead cost for a single animal vaccination averaged 22 cents. Bob was doing it for 9 cents per dose!

The vaccination program would ultimately inoculate three million animals a year for four years and save the entire animal herds of Northern Iraq. Because of this work, the animal population rose rapidly and people could buy safe meat once again. Kurds began buying animals because it was a safer investment than the Iraqi money. Bob wrote in one of his newsletters, "The Kurds face many crises—enemies around and enemies within, water shortages and no electricity — but one crisis was avoided by the livestock vaccination campaign. The work of providing cold vaccines has prevented a famine and restored a portion of the trade economy to the Kurdish people of Northern Iraq." The Kurdish will never forget the efforts of this mission while they were suffering. Bob said he heard Kurds everywhere saying, "God bless America."

Bob and I will never forget how God answered our prayers on the trip to Mosul. Isaiah 65:24 reads, "Before they call I will answer; while they are still speaking I will hear." Though for us, the experience was heart-pounding, God was in control. Whether he was blinding the eyes of the checkpoint agents or moving Jim's arm, he had a plan for getting those vaccinations to the Kurdish. For Bob and me, that experience allowed us to see the Lord at work.

I also learned something else about God. Think of it....Wrigley's chewing gum? God does have a great sense of humor.

CHAPTER TEN

COURAGE IN HELL

*For I am persuaded that neither death nor life, nor angels nor principalities
nor powers, nor things present nor things to come, nor height nor depth, nor
any other created thing, shall be able to separate us from the love of God
which is in Christ Jesus our Lord.* Romans 8:38-39

"We are placing premature babies, that should be in incu-
bators, into cardboard biscuit boxes on the ground!" These words
were spoken by Dr. Pat Huff of Fall City, Oregon. He and his wife
Carrie, a registered nurse, had just returned from the Rwanda
Refugee Camps of Goma, Zaire. Dr. Huff served as a medic in Viet
Nam and served nine different assignments with Northwest
Medical Teams. He found this place to be far more devastating,
chaotic, primitive, and rough than any situation he had ever
faced.

The doctor and his wife had been sent with other seasoned
volunteers such as Dr. Travis Cavens, and Dr. Earl Van
Volkinburg. The very best were sent because it was understood
that they would face some of the most horrible situations possible. Such conditions demanded hardy workers to face them. The
volunteers who went had served before in terrible places like the
Cambodian camps, Ethiopia, Sudan, and Somalia. However, they
were not prepared for what they would find at Goma, Zaire.

One of the doctors upon seeing the devastation of the people said, "This is what hell must be like." Dr. Cavens, in a
moment of reflection, said, "This is worse than hell."

In 1994, the Hutu tribe butchered over 500,000 people of
the Tutsi tribe in Rwanda. Eventually, the Tutsi Rebel Army
defeated the Hutu army and took power. In fear of reprisals, the
Hutus fled the country. It was reported that 2.5 million fled to

surrounding countries. Another 2.5 million fled their homes and became displaced within Rwanda. Of all who fled, 1.2 million would end up encamped on volcanic rock at Goma, Zaire.

Many people died before reaching Zaire. After arriving in the camps, many died from cholera and dysentery contracted by contaminated water supplies. By the time NWMT heard of the terrible sufferings, the mounting death toll was in the thousands. The situation prompted us to send the first of a number of teams to operate a field hospital in the middle of 400,000 refugees, more than ten times the amount of refugees we attempted to help in Cambodia when NWMT began.

The UN officials briefed us about the situation, explaining that there were so many people encamped that, if there was trouble, they would have a difficult time reaching us. What was left of the Hutu Army were encamped among the civilians. Officials feared there could be shooting and possibly rioting. Some agencies did not want to work inside the camp for fear of being caught in possible gunfire.

Uneasy feelings settled on my heart, when I learned that we could not count on help from the UN. However, I focused on our purpose — to save lives. Duly informed, the seasoned team decided to go into the camp. Because I was concerned for the team's safety, I visited the United States' military group working at Goma to tell them that NWMT members, fellow Americans, were working out in the large camp. I said, "If we need help, I hope the calvalry will come."

The officer laughed and said, "Sir, we will do our best to come to your aid, should it be needed." The reply gave me some comfort.

We arrived in Goma. From there, we drove about two miles up the road where we encountered a wall of people blocking the road. Slowly, we pushed through the throngs of people. It took us forty minutes to travel four miles.

Finally, we entered the camp, and witnessed the devastating effects of 400,000 people camping on volcanic rock. The smell of human waste was overpowering. The volcanic rock prevented the digging of latrines, and so not one was located among so many people. Everywhere we walked, we stepped in urine and feces.

People were milling about everywhere. A look of sadness and defeat settled on the face of every person we saw. No one smiled. An eerie quietude hung over the massive crowd. Thousands of small huts made from branches were propped up on the rock. One of the huts was covered with a little plastic; all the others had no guard against the rain. Such squalor had never been experienced by the seasoned volunteers.

The field hospital consisted of a few tents crammed with about 100 patients. The nurses and doctors could barely walk inside them. The tents also served as an outpatient hospital treating hundreds of people a day. The group quickly evaluated the hospital and supplies, and realized that more tents, medicine and food for patients were needed.

An awful feeling must be overcome, when a team realizes they are without enough supplies and are in the middle of nowhere. In the United States, medical volunteers have everything they need. In Goma, Zaire, the members just prayed they could get by until a new shipment came in. Necessity breeds creativity, however. Soon, Dennis Bean, a paramedic, was foraging around the camp for helpful items. Dennis had experienced similar situations with the team and knew that scrounging is an important part of the work. Other agencies might have medicines they did not need, and would give them away or trade for something they needed.

Once again as I had seen so many times over the years, the team quickly organized themselves and got busy saving lives. Paramedics Dennis Bean and Ron Hays, along with nurses Erda Fuller and Barb Scott, began attending to the very sick in the tents. These patients were admitted so they could be given an IV and antibiotics, and monitored for a few days. Dr. Cavens and Dr. Van Volkinburg examined the outpatients, who had lined up outside the hospital. Hundreds of them stood waiting to be helped.

Fortunately, volunteer Rwandan nurses had been found in the camp, and helped our team very much. When we were ordered to leave the camp at nights for our protection, the Rwandan nurses took over watching the patients.

An unusual person had accompanied me on the trip. A retired professional basketball player, Kermit Washington, from the Portland, Oregon Trailblazers desired to visit the disaster sight. I received a call from Kermit prior to leaving for my first visit. "I have been moved by the tragedy and would like to go with you, Ron," he said.

I answered, "We normally just take medical volunteers on this kind of trip."

Kermit said, "Ron, I would like to go see the needs for myself. Then, I will return and help raise money for your effort." His reply made sense.

"Sure, come along," I said. "You'll need to get all of your shots. Have you ever been to something this bad before?"

"No, but I grew up in a ghetto in D.C," he replied.

"Kermit, you may be shocked from the way people live in Africa in general."

He said, "Not me! I grew up in the ghetto. Nothing can shock me."

We landed in Nairobi, Kenya. After a few minutes of driving through the city, Kermit said, "I can't believe this! I had no idea these people lived like this!"

I replied, "This is one of the best cities in Africa."

When we arrived in Uganda, before flying into Goma, Zaire, Kermit was stunned by the poverty of people. When we walked into the camp, his reaction was greater. "I am shocked! In America, people gripe if they don't get the right color of clothing or a special food. These people have nothing and appreciate anything they are given!"

Such a response is typical from someone coming to a third world country for the first time. It is the same reaction whether it's Africa, India, the mountains or slums of Mexico, many Central and South American countries, or even many parts of Russia. It is always shocking to me, because of the contrast between our country and these.

A person from the worst ghetto in the United States would still be shocked by what they would see in Goma, Zaire. Some of the poorest areas in the United States are five times better than the places where NWMT does its work. Thus, it was no surprise to me when Kermit walked out into the camp with us, and could not believe the miserable state of the Rwandan people.

NBA Basketball star, Kermit Washington traveled, with NWMT to Rwanda. Here he attempts to make children laugh where there was no laughter in a camp of 400,000.

However, the poverty and desperation of the Rwandan people did not deter Kermit from his purpose. He found small ways to help while he was there. Some of the people were so sick, they could not leave their huts. Kermit helped us find these people and organized helpers to bring stretchers for carrying them. When he returned home, however, he began to make a big difference. His experience in Africa would have a lasting impact on Kermit, and countless others.

Kermit visited the slums of Nairobi, Kenya where several million people lived in extreme poverty. No jobs are available, and there is very little on which to survive. Kermit decided to help them. He returned home on a separate trip, raised money for medical supplies and returned to the slum. After finding a clinic, he donated medicines and organized volunteers. Now, he travels to the clinic up to six times a year. Some people see poverty, but do nothing. Kermit did do something about it, though. Through his efforts, many people are receiving help.

Compassion

When Jesus landed and saw a large crowd, he had compassion on them and healed their sick. Matthew 14:14

"Please, bring me a spinal tap needle!" Dr. Travis Cavens shouted. Nurse Barb Scott ran to the supply tent. Dr. Cavens, chairman of the board of NWMT, prepared a ten-year-old Rwandan girl for a spinal tap. A board lain across two saw horses outside the clinic tent was used as an examining table. The girl was moved to it. "She may have spinal meningitis, but I need to tap her spine to find out," said Dr. Cavens. "Kermit, would you hold her on her side while I do this?" Kermit's six-foot, ten-inch frame towered above Dr. Cavens as his big hands gently held the young girl's body.

The exam confirmed Dr. Caven's diagnosis. She had spinal meningitis. "I am not sure she will be alive tomorrow. We will have to see," said Dr. Cavens.

He put an IV in the little girl's limp arm and began giving her the medicine that could help her. She was burning up with fever and was nearly unconscious. Kermit and Dennis Bean stood by watching with concern for the child as Dr. Cavens finished and was ready to go on to the hundreds of other sick people. "Please be careful with the IV and take her to a tent," Dr. Cavens asked.

Dennis picked up the lifeless body of the young girl, while Kermit held the IV bottle high. They carried her to a tent and gently placed her on a cot.

I walked over to where Dr. Cavens was attending to more patients. The line of mothers holding babies or young children was almost overwhelming. There must have been 150 mothers waiting for the doctor to examine their children. How could one pediatrician see all of these? I wondered what Dr. Cavens thought as he looked at the long line. Like when helping with other disasters, he cared for them one at a time. Concern and compassion was shown to each mother and child as they were examined.

I was bunking with Dr. Cavens. That night, as we sat on our bunks, reflecting, I asked him, "Do you realize, in addition to the ten-year-old girl with spinal meningitis, how many children you examined today?"

He replied, "No, I don't know."

"Travis," I answered, "you saw 216 babies! This is an amazing feat, because they were all very sick." At home, Dr. Cavens might see as many as 30 children in one day at his pediatric clinic in Longview, Washington.

Dr. Travis Cavens in 1994 seeing over 200 children among the Rwandan refugees in a simple, makeshift field hospital located in a camp of over 400,000 people in what is now Congo. Photo, Ben Brink, *The Oregonian*.

I looked over at my friend. He was weeping in a way I had never seen before. Deep sobs were overflowing from a broken heart. I placed my hand on his knee. When he regained composure, he explained. "I am crying for the sick babies I saw today who might not be alive when I return in the morning. I am crying for the 130 children who were still in line when we had to leave tonight." The United Nations required us to leave the camp at a certain time each night. Though many of the workers did not want to leave, they needed the rest, as well as the protection.

Dr. Cavens was running a race to save lives. Though many battles were won, so many were also lost. It is hard to remain positive in the midst of such circumstances, at times. Only very strong hearts can manage it.

Several years later, I talked to Travis about that night. After evaluating the evening, Travis discovered there were other factors that caused him to break down. I asked him to send me his journal which eloquently shares the heart of a compassionate man.

"Dear Ron,

Having served in the dreadful refugee camps of Thailand, Iraq, and Ethiopia, I was surprised at my emotional reaction on the first clinic day in the Rwanda camp at Mawenzie. That night, as you recall, I broke down crying, not with just some tears running down my cheeks. I was sobbing! I hadn't done that since I was a small child, and it puzzled me.

I suspect it was the stress of finally flying in to Rwanda, organizing the medical aspects of the team, and then seeing those 216 patients on that first day. I could not believe I had seen so many. It was true I was concerned about that ten-year-old with spinal meningitis and worried about all those children I did not get to see, but I believe there were other reasons.

What set me off that evening when we were together in our room was that I started reliving an encounter that day with a little girl. She was about nine years old with a pretty face and confident manner. She was barefoot and dressed in a dirty, brown dress. On her frail back she carried her little brother who was about three years old. He was terribly dehydrated due to vomiting and diarrhea and could barely raise his head.

Through my translator, I told the little girl that we needed to keep the child at our clinic and treat him. But her parents were not with her, and evidently she had firm orders to just bring him to the doctor for medicine and then return. I argued with her some more, but she wouldn't change her mind. I ended up giving her oral rehydration solution packets and an antibiotic for her brother and let her leave.

That evening I was worrying if I had done the right thing. Should I have been more forceful and kept the boy, against the sister's resistance and the parents' permission. I thought, "That little boy is going to die." I was overwhelmed with a profound sadness. I suspect he became a symbol to me of all the tragedy I had seen that day. Thank goodness, you were the only one that saw me cry, for it wouldn't have been reassuring for the rest of the team to see the medical leader falling apart. But you are a good friend.

My spirits vastly improved as we were organized and had successes. We were able to move the not-so-sick men out of one of the big tents and make it into a pediatric ward. A very dehydrated girl was brought in late one afternoon. I ordered IV fluids for her and soon the nurse had the IV going. But we had to leave for the night as usual and trust that our patients would survive without us.

The next morning I was on my knees going from patient to patient on the plastic floor and picked up the chart of that little girl. I looked at who was in her place and began to get angry, because it wasn't the same girl. I was about to take some nurse to task as doctors often do, when I took a closer look and realized that this indeed was the same child. I hadn't recognized her, because her eyes that had been so sunken now looked bright and alert. Her skin no longer tented up when you pulled on it, but felt soft. With fluid and care, she had bloomed like a flower in the desert. And so I was elated.

I, of course, had many other times of elation, but I remember specifically just a few, such as the boy who was brought to the roadside clinic with pneumonia. It was so easy to hear the extensive fluid in his lungs with the stethoscope, something we don't often experience in our private practice where pneumonia is diagnosed so early and often only with an X-ray. But this child had bad pneumonia. He was breathing so hard the skin was sucking in between his ribs. We had no way to hospitalize him and put him in an oxygen tent. I gave him a shot of the antibiotic, Rocephin, and asked his mother to bring him back the next day. She did, and I was exulted. He no longer was in any respiratory distress and was actually smiling. In my excitement, I tried to get my colleagues to come see him. But they weren't very interested since he really looked good now and they had to see to their own patients. I realized that this little victory would be shared by just God and me alone.

These trips have changed our lives, of course. A pivotal time was after I returned from Thailand. The local daily paper wanted to publish a five-part series that I had written about my adventures there. In those articles I had determined that I would write about my Christian faith as being an integral part of my going to help. I had decided that it was time in my life to publicly proclaim that I was a Christian, and was concerned that the newspaper editor would take out the Christian references and use only the "interesting" items. So I stipulated in a letter to the publisher, Ted Natt, that I would submit the articles if they didn't change a word. He wrote back that he changes the words of even his best reporters. I did proceed to submit the articles and was pleased to find that not one word was changed. The Christian witness was intact."

Travis is an example of many people who have chosen to turn from seeking satisfaction for themselves and instead, have sought to help others. In the midst of trials, they exhibited bravery. How courageous to not want to cry in front of the other team members because he was the leader. What Travis may have not realized was that other team members were likely in their rooms crying at the same time. Many of these volunteers worked under harsh conditions all day trying to help as many people as possible, though they wanted to break under the weight of so many tragic cases. When the day was over, some would walk to some lonely and quiet place to cry over the events of the day.

The emotional trials are accompanied by physical ones. Often, the volunteers must work without adequate supplies or helpers. Rather than giving up, they fight with everything within them to save lives. They sleep in uncomfortable quarters and eat unfamiliar food. They often get dysentery, but they do not slow down in their work.

Their lives are never the same. In the case of Dr. Travis Cavens, not only his life, but that of his entire family, was transformed. Phyllis and Travis once wrote, "We could have ignored any subsequent calls to serve with Northwest Medical Teams and instead pursued the life of becoming rich in which we joined the country club, built a beautiful view home on a hill, and became self-centered bores. But after experiencing the joy of seeing a baby return from the brink of death by what we did, we knew our lives had to be more than that."

Their lives became centered on important matters: God, family, their medical practice and Northwest Medical Teams. Their relationship with God deepened. This occurrence is common among volunteers. Perhaps because it is in the midst of suffering where one has a great sense of God's presence. To look into the face of someone who is reaching out for life, the presence of the One who created that person is near. The presence of God is powerful, and it almost always changes the person who encounters it.

As a result of their experiences, Travis and Phyllis changed the priorities for their family. They taught their children about the family motto: Cavens stands for kindness. Words aren't always sufficient, however. Travis and Phyllis also demonstrated kindness in their daily actions. The children have followed suit. Sonja became a nurse, and Derek works in a home for developmentally delayed adults.

Both Phyllis and Travis accompanied NWMT on many outreaches. When a disaster would strike somewhere in the world, people in the Cavens' community would ask them if they were going. People participated in the Cavens' mission by dropping off medical supplies at their office to pass on to NWMT.

Today, these two Samaritans are still leaving the comfort of their home to help people who suffer. In 1998, Phyllis led the first medical team to give aid to the victims of Hurricane Mitch in Honduras. Months later, Travis led the first team to aid the refugees pouring out of Kosovo into Albania. The effort and need continue in these two areas today.

The morning after sitting with my friend Travis, we returned to the camp. I wondered what each medical volunteer was thinking. Perhaps they were wondering if their patients had made it through the night.

When we arrived, the volunteers divided up to seek out

their personal patients in the tents. It was a joy to see their faces as they checked on those who had improved. The day before, a patient was near death, and today he can sit up and take food. I often felt as if I've witnessed many Lazarus events, where life returns where death once reigned.

For Dr. Cavens, however, the joyous occasion was not meant to be. As he checked on the little ten-year-old girl who had spinal meningitis, he discovered she had died. The grief was overwhelming. Workers carried her small, lifeless body from the tent. Nurse Fuller sobbed out, "It isn't fair! It isn't fair!" Dennis Bean put his arms around her and they paused to share the grief.

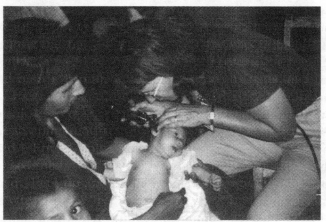

Dr. Phyllis Cavens helps a baby during the aftermath of Hurricane Mitch in Honduras in November, 1998. Photo, Dr. Phyllis Cavens.

It is never easy to lose one of these little children. We could only commit her to the arms of a loving God, knowing she would never again suffer pain and hunger. Then, the volunteers prepared themselves for another day of caring for hundreds who were still alive.

Burial Preparations

Going to Pilate, he asked for Jesus' body. Then he took it down, wrapped it in linen cloth and placed it in a tomb cut in the rock, one in which no one had yet been laid. Luke 23:52,53

I am confident that Heaven exists, and that it is a wonderful place. Why, then, do I grieve over the death of someone? In analyzing my feelings, I have discovered that I grieve for those who are left behind. When I lost my beloved parents, I knew they were safe with the Lord. Yet, I felt a deep grief knowing I would never talk with them or visit with them again on earth. Though acceptance comes, the grief does not disappear.

Many sad scenes play in my memory. Groups of mothers rocking back and forth, disbelief and despair evident on their faces, as they sobbed over losing a child. When I saw a father grieving, my heart would feel as if it was ripping apart. To me, that is the saddest picture of all. Perhaps it is because I am a father myself. Perhaps because the show of emotion in a father, who was taught that crying is unacceptable, makes it more striking.

I will never forget a young Ethiopian father who was told that his son had died. He sat on the ground, folded his arms over his head, and tried very hard not to cry. But his pain was too much, and he could no longer contain the tears welling up inside. He wept as he rocked back and forth. The expression on his face begged, "Please, not my son!" I wept for this young father. Though the son was safe in the arms of God, the father would always feel the loss.

For the Rwandan refugee, death was often denied certain dignities. Each day, bodies were stacked along the road, as we drove to camp. The people who died during the night were rolled up in matting and lain along the road for pick-up and mass burial.

After seeing these bodies day after day, I questioned, "Who put these bodies along the road?" The realization of the answer swept over me. Loved ones did this! A father, mother, sister, brother or friend were the ones who lovingly rolled the body in the matting. I imagined them carrying the body to the road, sobbing with grief.

Rwandan refugees were denied even the small comforts of

a proper burial. These people were placing the bodies along the road to be picked up for mass burial. They would not attend any funeral service or ever even know where the loved one was buried. Perhaps, for many of these people, the death of their loved one would be without closure.

I put myself in the place of a refugee. Could I carry my wife, Jean, my son, Bill, my daughters, Sheri and Dawn, and roll their bodies in matting? Could I place them alongside a roadway, and then, walk away knowing they would be buried in an unknown place? As I pictured each one of them, my heart grew so heavy that I cried. These people were suffering a tragedy that words could not describe. My fervor was renewed to do all we could to relieve their suffering. God would have me do no less.

Good Samaritans

But a Samaritan, as he traveled, came where the man was; and when he saw him, he took pity on him. He went to him and bandaged his wounds, pouring on oil and wine. Luke 10:33,34

Each day the drive to the camp along the Goma road entailed pushing through a sea of people. Sick people beside the road awaited their fates patiently. The pain evident in their faces reminded us of the man injured along the road in the story of the good Samaritan. Jesus praised the good Samaritan for stopping to help the man, when others would not. We did not want to be the "others" who would not stop.

In response, we decided to install a tent clinic along the road, and split our team so these people could receive care. With help from local nationals, a sight was chosen. Before the tent could be raised, considerable time was spent clearing the human waste from the area. The smell was overpowering. I pitched in. After working for awhile, Paramedic Ron Hays yelled out, "Watch out, Ron, you're about to step in some!" For a brief moment, in the middle of all the tragedy around us, we all laughed at Ron's joke.

The joke caused me to consider the situation. I felt for these people. They had no privacy when they needed to eliminate.

Nor was there any kind of toilet that could seemingly be made because of the volcanic rock. They had been stripped of their dignity.

Dr. Pat Huff and his wife, nurse Carrie, organized the tent set-up and supplies. Before they were ready, people were already lining up, and within a few moments of the medical team's final preparations, hundreds of people were in line to receive medical attention. Our team kept reminding themselves that they were to help one person at a time. Otherwise, the tasks would be overwhelming. One family walked up right away with the father on a stretcher. Dr. Huff had the painful task of telling the family that the father had died. Though such a beginning did not appear promising, many others were saved because of the clinic.

The group of volunteers truly acted as good Samaritans. They cared for each person as though he or she was the only one they had to help. An elderly lady collapsed on the ground outside the tent, before she could see the doctor. Nurse Carrie Huff immediately went to her side and ministered to the lady under a tree along the road. Carrie held the IV bottle in one hand, allowing the life-saving solution to enter the woman's system, while gently stroking the lady's head. The picture is a treasure to my memo-

The author helping establish a roadside clinic for the thousands who passed daily on the Goma Road during the Rwandian crisis. Photo, NWMT.

ry. The woman lived thanks to the care.

After we got the clinic tent up and operating, I wandered around the area. I soon made an exciting discovery. Near the tent, and next to the road, there was a hole in the ground. The opening was about three feet by five feet. I got down and peered into the hole. I could not see the back of the large cavern below the ground. It was a volcanic blow-hole. "A latrine can be built," I thought to myself.

I asked one of the volunteer nationals to search for carpenters among the people walking on the road. A few moments later, several were found. I told them I would pay them if they could collect enough wood to build a two-hole latrine. They agreed, and within three hours we had the first latrine in the whole area. A feeling of deep satisfaction spread through me. Then I chuckled at myself. I never thought I would get so excited over a latrine!

The Common Thread

My command is this: Love each other as I have loved you. Greater love has no one than this, that he lay down his life for his friends. John 15:12,13

During the thirty days the first team worked in Goma, the small team of volunteers treated 25,000 patients. Though they lost some, thousands of others were saved. Often without adequate medicine, space, and medical equipment, the group worked with what they possessed to bring healing to the masses.

Once again, the faithfulness of God was easily observed through the works he performed through NWMT volunteers. Watching the medical team members work reminded me of our compassionate Christ. The Bible stories that describe Jesus stopping to heal people time after time, became so real. Christ demonstrated His compassion. Now, it was clear that He wants us to demonstrate that same kind of compassion today. As volunteers work with their gentle hands, I catch a glimpse of how Jesus is still working miracles through the hands of His servants.

The composition of the first team caused me to consider the true family Jesus desires us to be. The team consisted of people who attend various denominational churches. Lutherans,

Catholics, Baptists, and some from non-denominational churches all worked together side by side. How pleasing this unity must
be to God.

Compassion was not only exhibited by medical volunteers.
As our medical volunteers reached out to Rwandan refugees, high
up in the mountains of Mexico, non-medical volunteers were
building a health house or constructing a clean water system for
an Indian village. Each one is a good Samaritan.

"What type of people volunteer for Northwest Medical
Teams?" The question has been asked many times. The best
answer I have heard has been that of my good friend, Don Clark,
now an ABC Television anchor for a Bakersfield, California news
station. He once said at a banquet, "Some people go out of a deep
Christian faith that God asks them to care for the poor. Some go
out of humanitarian reasons. They want to care for their fellow
man. Then there is the one who is like a person that hears a cry
from below in a river. They just jump in without time to think.
They don't always know why they go, they just feel they need to
go. The common thread that weaves through these people is compassion. They are all good Samaritans."

CHAPTER ELEVEN

RUNNING THE COURSE SET BEFORE THEM

Therefore, since we are surrounded by such a great cloud of witnesses, let us throw off everything that hinders and the sin that so easily entangles, and let us run with perseverance the race marked out for us. Hebrews 12:1

Who am I? Where did I come from? Where am I going? Is there any meaning to my life? All of us must evaluate and answer these questions sometime in our lives. I settled the first three questions in 1965, age 27. The last question took me many years more to answer.

After 1965, I knew who I was because I chose to follow Christ. I am a child of God through Jesus Christ who paid the price for me. I knew I was created by a loving God so that answered where I came from. I knew I was going to heaven one day to be with Him when I died and that I would also be with all my loved ones who chose to follow Christ. That answered where I was going. However, for years I wondered about the last question, "Is there any meaning to my life?" I discovered many other followers of Christ struggling with the same question.

In 1979, when I led that first team to help the Cambodians, I discovered the answer to that last question. Over the years, it has been confirmed again and again. Before Cambodia, I did not know many people who had answered the question. After Cambodia, I came into contact with hundreds of people who have settled the question. I am blessed by being involved with works that help people discover the significance of their lives.

What is the answer to this difficult question? It is a simple answer, but sometimes it is difficult to practice. Summed up in a word, the answer is "servitude." The definition of a servant is "one who does for others with no gain for self." I have had the privilege of working with many servants at Northwest Medical Teams over many years. Each member has settled the question of the meaning for their own lives, bringing a deep peace.

Northwest Medical Teams continues to be true to its original intent, to reach out to hurting people all over the world. I would like to share with you some of the interesting stories and testimonies of those who have witnessed how volunteering to help those less fortunate has changed their lives.

One of the largest earthquakes of our century occurred in Armenia, then called Soviet Armenia, in 1988. The earthquake's upheaval leveled two major cities. The city of Leninakan was nearly destroyed. Thousands of the 250,000 people perished. In the city of Spitak, not one building remained standing. Of the 45,000 people within its limits, 22,000 people living at the center of the city died. In all, it was estimated that 120,000 to 150,000 people died from the disaster.

In response, NWMT organized an orthopedic surgery team to perform surgeries on victims who suffered from fractures. We also hoped to bring medical equipment and supplies to their hospitals, because we learned they had very little. Once again, we were without means of transportation both for the team and the donated supplies, until Flying Tigers Airline donated a 747.

When we arrived, several "firsts" were accomplished through our effort. We became the first Americans to ever be granted permission to enter the Soviet Union without a visa. We became the first American medical team to work in Soviet Armenia. We were on the first Boeing 747 to ever land in that part of the Soviet Union.

The landing of the 747 was an event for both those on and off the aircraft. People lined the runway to catch a glimpse of the huge airplane landing. Once we landed, however, we were informed that there was no gang plank that could reach the 747. We had to carefully climb down a ladder to the ground. The airport also had no equipment to unload the cargo. It had to be unloaded by hand. It took 15 military trucks to transport all the equipment we had brought for the hospital. The team then boarded buses provided for us, and left with the trucks to the hospital where we would work in the capital of Yerevan.

Jean accompanied me on this trip, and together we experienced something grand. Dr. Jerry Becker and I were working in a tent out in the parking lot of the hospital. I heard a car drive up and became curious to see who it was. I walked out of the tent and almost bumped into Mother Teresa. She had arrived for a visit to the hospital.

I had the great privilege of spending five minutes alone with this unbelievable woman. She only stood a little taller than my waist. Though she appeared frail, her face shone with a radiance that could only have been the love of Christ flowing through her. When I tried to praise her, her hands would immediately come together in prayer fashion and she would say, "Glory to God." Shortly, after I had that special time with her, Jean had a chance to meet her and someone got a picture of Mother Teresa kissing a medallion and giving it to Jean. Jean has the treasure to this day.

A popular bumper sticker reads, "He who has the most toys wins," which defines the measure of success for many people. Yet, if the bumper sticker is true, then Mother Teresa was a loser. The woman of God had nothing. However, now she has more riches than this world could ever give. Proverbs 19:17 reads, "He who is kind to the poor lends to the Lord, and he will reward him for what he has done." God is rewarding her for the many years of kindness she bestowed upon the poor.

Our surgery teams performed many operations on earthquake victims. What was heartbreaking was seeing people on carts in the hallways waiting for surgery with severely broken bones and without the aid of pain medication.

One morning, Jean made rounds with our doctor. They went into a room where a woman was suffering from a ghastly open wound in her foot. She was lying in a small bed. The doctor examined her, and then said that the packing for the wound needed changing. Unfortunately, there was no pain medication. The pain must have been excruciating.

After the painful experience of having her packing changed,

she wanted to thank our people. She grabbed the surgeon's hand
and shook it. She then motioned for Jean to come closer. Jean
responded with her hand, thinking she wanted to shake her hand
also. Instead, she grasped it, pulled Jean closer and began to kiss
the back of her hand and up her arm. Jean was completely overcome by the outpouring of gratitude. The tears were coursing
down the lady's cheeks as Jean knelt and wrapped her arms
around her. Jean leaned over and kissed her on the forehead.
They both wept together.

Jean later said, "I believe our teams did more for human
relations than all of the politicians put together." I agree. The love
of Christ overflows political divisions. Disregarding race, religion,
or place of birth, it unifies the human race so that all people are
the neighbor whom we are called to love.

Kenya

In 1993, Somalian refugees poured across the border of
Kenya. Famine and war was ravaging the country of Somalia.
Over 250,000 people fled its horrors, and ended up encamped
near Wajir, Kenya. Wajir appears to be a stop on the way to
nowhere. Someone said, "Wajir is not the last place on earth, but
you can see it from there."

The streets were dirt. Many of us were reminded of old
western movies that depicted the frontier of America as vast country, dotted with dusty, little towns. The people of the region are
poor, carving out a living by farming and raising livestock. The
Somalis who streamed into the area were not welcome, and they
were forced to camp away from the town.

The refugees built thatched huts, and tried to live on a starvation diet. Most became severely malnourished and many suffered from cholera and dysentery. The children suffered from
these ailments, as well as dehydration. Many died.

Dr. Don Walker and Jane Walker, a registered nurse, were
one of the first couples to respond to the Somalia crisis. When a
medical team was needed on short notice, which is a usual occurrence, they were ready to go. Don and Jane felt that their experi-

ence in Somalia was the one they will always remember the most. There were so many people to help and they could not help them fast enough. As always, they began helping one person at a time.

Shortly after starting work there, a woman was brought into the clinic. They discovered that the lady had been bitten by one of the many poisonous snakes in the area. Because we had no snake anti-venom, Don and Jane decided to take her to the local hospital. However, the hospital often caused the deaths of its patients, rather than cured them. It was dirty and little medication or equipment was available. Disturbingly, they also found that the hospital would not serve Somali refugees. Hospital officials informed Don and Jane that they had no snake serum, but it was a lie.

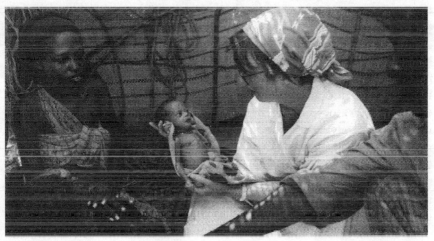

RN Barbara Scott looks after a malnourished child during the refugee crisis in Somolia. Photo courtesy of Ben Brink, *The Oregonian.*

Don and Jane then took the woman to a local Muslim mosque where they were told that snake serum was available. Because the woman was Muslim, Don and Jane felt confident she would receive the needed help.

The next day, Jane and other team members were working in the tent clinic. The shrill chant from a burial site nearby interrupted their work. The mourning of the relatives was also audible. Jane inquired about the death, and discovered it was the woman with the snake bite. The Muslim Church had not given her the life-saving serum, because the woman was over 40 and had already had her children.

How could life be of such little value? Every life is precious and sacred. Yet, it is difficult to understand and judge the ideas of another culture.

The Somali experience changed Dr. Don and Jane Walker's lives very much. Together, they decided to "downsize" their lives so they could help more people in need. Jane served as a director on the board of Northwest Medical Teams for six years. When her term was up, Dr. Don took her place on the board. Seeing people like the lady who died of a snake bite for lack of serum inscribed something very important in their minds. "Every life is precious and every life is of great value."

Another couple who worked together in Kenya was Dr. Dan MacDougall, a pediatrician, and Dr. Lindsey MacDougall, a pathologist. Lindsey set up an excellent laboratory for testing blood and urine samples. No other laboratory facility existed. With a laboratory, doctors could diagnose illnesses easier and more accurately.

Dan held clinics out in the camps. One day, some people told us there was a large group of sick people who were living about fifty miles away in the bush. Dr. Dan wanted to take a small medical team to them. The local officials told us it was dangerous to travel there because bandits roamed the area. In spite of these warnings, the team attempted the mission anyway. In response, the local police station sent four armed policemen to escort the team.

We left early in the morning, using two 4-wheel drive vehicles. I drove the lead vehicle and was directed where to go by one of our national workers. The police told me to drive quickly and not to stop, which would make it difficult for bandits to approach us. The road was soft dirt and we traveled at about 45 miles per hour. Frequently, we slowed down to avoid hitting camels, giraffes, and donkeys.

After traveling about forty miles, there were no signs of civilization anywhere. Therefore, I was surprised when I spotted a man walking on the dirt road. "Where is he going?" I thought. "There is no destination out here — there is nothing." I pitied the man, because it was so hot. As we passed him, my eyes met his. I could see he was weak and was having trouble walking.

As the wheels of the vehicle rolled over another 500 feet, many thoughts passed through my mind. I remembered the injured man in Jesus' parable, and the good Samaritan who helped him. "On the other hand," I thought, "if we stop for this man, it would put us behind schedule. After all, hundreds of people were waiting for help just a few miles ahead, and this was just one man."

I still felt compelled to stop. I did it without considering the possibility that the man was part of a clever trick for the bandits to stop and ambush us. I just had to stop. I jumped out of my vehicle and asked Dr. Dan to examine the man. He motioned for a translator. The policemen jumped out immediately and set up a perimeter security.

The man slumped to the ground as we approached him. Dr. Dan diagnosed the man with malaria. Even though food had been available to the man, he had not eaten for the last four days. Dan gave him water and all the medicine he would need to get well.

We returned to our vehicles and continued. I felt good. I knew we had done the right thing. Again I was reminded of the story of the good Samaritan. Perhaps the travelers who passed by the beaten man also had somewhere important to go. Yet, God impressed upon me the importance of each individual. He assured me there would be a way to accomplish all that was needed, even if I stopped for this one man.

We arrived in the small village of Tarbaj and set up a clinic under an acacia tree. The medical team set up stools in a circle for the patients and doctors or nurses. Word quickly went out about the medical team arriving and within minutes there was a line of people waiting to be examined. Many mothers came with their sick children. The people were so anxious to get into the clinic that policemen were called to control the crowd.

One common problem was infection from thorns. Long, thorny bushes were everywhere, and when a person stepped on one, the thorn would go deep into the foot. Dr. Allen Henderson, who was at retirement age, decided to take a translator and go out into the bush. Dr. Henderson believed that there were sick people who could not walk to the clinic; he was right. Because of his insight, many people were treated in their huts. Dr. Henderson treated one woman whose foot was so infected and swollen that she could not walk. The infection would have caused her to lose her foot if they had not treated her soon.

While I was at the clinic, Nurse Mary Sue Richards asked

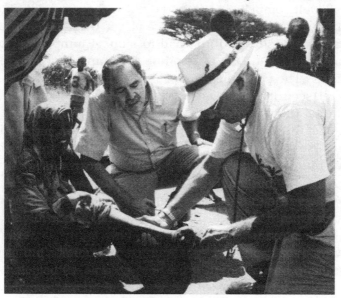

Ron Post watching as Dr. Allen Henderson treats an infected foot at the hut of a Somali woman. Photo NWMT.

me to help retrieve one of these thorns out of a young boy's foot. His foot was swollen and infected. Mary Sue used a needle to probe the foot. Then she said, "Ron, there it is. Grab it with your fingers and pull it out!" I grabbed it and pulled. As it came out, I was amazed at the length. It was three inches long. The young boy never uttered a sound of pain.

Not long after setting up, Dan called me over to show me a baby brought in by a young mother. The baby was just skin and bones. She was severely dehydrated. Dan said, "It will be difficult to save the baby."

In the United States, the baby would be put on a life support system, until she was stronger, and the baby would likely live. But we were in the bush. Dale Burkholz, a television cameraman, had been videoing the unfolding story. Dan looked into the camera, and said, "This baby might not live out the day." Then, he mixed up a solution, called ORS (Oral Rehydration Solution). Next to penicillin, ORS is one of the greatest discoveries for third world countries. The majority of children in these countries die from dehydration caused by malnutrition and parasites. When a ten cent pack of ORS is mixed with a liter of water, it gives a child the potassium and electrolytes he or she needs to recover from dehydration. Millions of children near death have recovered after taking ORS.

After mixing the solution, Dan showed the young mother how to use an eye dropper to give her baby the ORS and antibiotics. The young mother was instructed to sit down and give the baby all the solution.

Just before lunch, I spotted the young mother with the sick baby. She was sitting on the ground holding her baby, but I could see she was not giving the baby the ORS solution. I told Dan, who was very busy with patients. He replied, "It is extremely important to get that solution down the baby, or she will die." We had learned that in this people's religion, if they thought a child was too far gone, they would let him or her die. They felt it was the will of God.

I asked the mother to allow me to hold the baby. I sat down, took the eye dropper and started forcing the solution down the baby's throat. The baby could not swallow on her own. This is common for someone who is severely dehydrated. I put the solution in her mouth and rubbed the baby's throat, allowing it to drain down into her tummy. The baby was staring up at me with glazed eyes. I could see what a beautiful child she was and my heart went out to her.

After about ten minutes of forcing the solution down the baby, Mary Sue came over to check on her. She took the baby and checked her pulse. She told me the pulse was fading. I was feeling helpless. In that short few minutes, I had formed a bond with the child. As Mary Sue held the baby, I reached over and placed my arms around them and prayed.

A crowd started forming around us as though they knew this child was dying. Several people stepped forward and tried to close the baby's eyes as you do after someone dies.

I pushed them back. The baby was not dead! The community leader came up and said, "The baby is dead."

I answered vehemently, "The baby is not dead!"

It disturbed me as more people tried to close the baby's eyes. I said "No! God does not want this child to die!"

Mary Sue forced more antibiotic down the baby's throat, but she grew worse. Dan came over to check the baby and said, "Ron, the baby is near death. The pulse is very weak."

I cried out, "No!" Then, the baby died. The weeping mothers snatched the baby out of Mary Sue's arms and a line of wailing women began carrying the baby away. I was stunned. I put my head on my knees, covered my face, and sobbed. I got up and walked away where I could be alone. I cried out, "Why Lord? Why did this child have to die?"

I was devastated. I had seen dead children during many trips around the world. Yet, I had never held a baby and bonded with her, just to have her die. I later understood what our medical volunteers must have felt so many times when they lost a child after trying to save him or her. The pain was great. It could not have been greater if it had been my own child or grandchild. I just could not release this child.

Mary Sue came over to where I was and put her arm around me and we both cried. Then, Dan came over to where we were. He said, "Ron, I see children die and it's always difficult. I know this child is in the presence of our Lord right now. She is healed. I do not know why. Maybe the Lord wants us to see the pain, so we will not forget how many children in our world need help."

As we prayed, I asked the Lord to reveal to me why this child died. I know He will in His time. I will never forget that baby. The baby's face is vivid and clear in my memory, and the

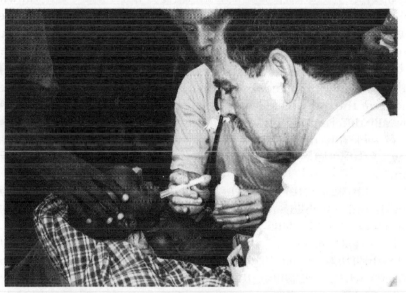

The author helps nurse Mary Sue Richards give a Somolian baby oral rehydration solution in an attempt to save the baby from dehydration. Moments later the baby died and its death left an everlasting impression on Ron.
Photo, NWMT.

pain of her death is still sharp and fresh in my heart.

Perhaps Dan is right. Maybe God wants me to remember the child. Her death rattled my innermost being. The shock of it reminds me how important it is to save as many little ones in our world as possible. I want to see that child again one day when I am called home to heaven.

The United States

Oscar's teeth were black, and the teacher could not tell if they were fillings or teeth. She noticed he had an awkward time chewing food, not knowing on which side to chew. The food would often fall out of his mouth. He constantly had a mucous running from his nose and other children did not want to sit by him. No one wanted to be near him at lunch time. Yet, she said Oscar was the sweetest boy. However, she added that he was struggling with his grades.

One day, our dental unit pulled into the school grounds and Oscar was seen by Dr. Lee Emery, one of our volunteer dentists. Dr. Emery said that Oscar had multiple dental abscesses in his mouth. They removed the non-salvageable, abscessed teeth on the initial visit. On subsequent visits they were able to restore and treat the other teeth. After these visits, his teacher said, "He's a totally different kid. It's been a life-changing thing for him. He's never sick any more. He is doing so much better in his studies now. I truly believe it's all because the toxicity is out of his system."

The van returns to the school the first Friday of every month and the children look forward to the visit with the dentists. The teacher said, "This is literally a god-send for these children and I'm really grateful."

In 1988, I was struck by the growing number of our own citizens who were falling through the cracks of our health care system. In most states, if a family of four made over $12,000 to $13,000 a year, they did not qualify for state health assistance. Yet, a family of four cannot pay for health care at the current cost. If they get sick, they may be able to pay medical bills, but dental health was beyond what they could afford. This group of people were growing by over a million people a year in our country.

Perhaps we could attract enough dentists, hygienists and dental assistants to volunteer their time so we could provide free dental care. By faith, we campaigned for funds to purchase and outfit a mobile health van. We wanted a mobile unit that could go to many places. Many people, such as migrant workers who pick crops, did not have transportation to come to a stationary clinic.

MOEX Corporation, located nearby, made mobile health units. They had a 35' unit that could provide two rooms telescoping out on each side which would give us room to install two dental rooms and an X-ray room. Thanks to a number of corporations, foundations and individuals, we raised the funds to get the unit.

The call went out for volunteers and the response was wonderful. One of the first volunteers was Dr. Lee Emery. He was on an errand one day and saw our building and sign. He had heard about our mission and wondered if there was a place for him to serve. He came in and met with our medical director, Dr. John Lassater, who was just getting the mobile van ready. Dr. Emery immediately signed up to work a day each month on the van.

The first outreaches with the van were to help the many migrant camps. None of these people made enough picking crops to afford dental care. Children's teeth were rotten and many were infected. Dr. Emery, being a pediatric dentist, began helping children like Oscar. It was easy to see this man cared very much for children.

I asked Dr. Emery later why he continued doing this work. "First of all, it's selfish," he responded. "It makes me feel good!" He told me it had become a way of life for him. He looked forward to getting on the van each time. He said, "I know that the kids I give help to is the last stop; that is, if I don't do it, it most probably won't get done." He loves the fact he can take all the training he received and now give back to the community.

I had been concerned as to whether enough people would care enough to help. The response from individuals, civic groups, and corporations has been so good, we decided to add more units. Ten years after putting that first mobile clinic on the road, four units are being utilized with two more sheduled to go before long. These units are going to schools, migrant camps, churches, homeless shelters, street kids, and other places where the working poor need help. We will have the ability to care for 42,000 patients per year.

I was very pleased that my son, Bill, became a coordinator for one of the new mobile vans. He represents the next generation of people who are finding meaning in their lives by helping others. I am very proud of him for taking that step.

Our local Rotary Club wanted to help people in the Tigard community and discovered that the mobile van was a great vehicle, no pun intended, for the endeavor. We started a program called, "Dental Check Day." A van is sent to a local school where low income children are invited to a dental check. Dental sealant is provided to protect them from cavities. Rotary Club members volunteered to help out including our dentist who belongs to the club. When a child was found to have problems, he or she was referred to our van on a dental day or was seen in a local dentist office. The City of Tigard, Oregon, is very appreciative and proud

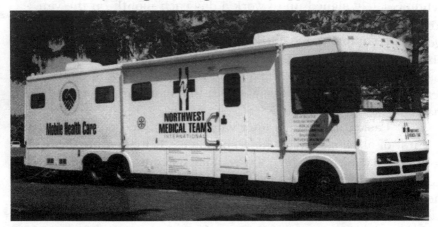

One of five Northwest Medical Teams Mobile Health Vans. Photo, NWMT.

of the Rotary Club for taking on this project.

One of the people who became involved on "Dental Check Day," was Laurie Johnson. Laurie, a dental hygienist, was asked by her employer to help out one day, eight years ago. That day turned into many days as the years passed by. She began helping once a month. Laurie had hidden herself away in her successful private practice for 25 years. Unaware of the pain and suffering so many were going through, she was shocked to see it in her own community. Many people suffered from dental neglect, dealing with terrible pain. Yet, people accepted it as part of their life because there seemed to be no viable alternative.

After years of helping on the van, Laurie was bothered by the lack of education people had about dental prevention. Many of the people who were helped did not have access to good educational materials to prevent most dental problems. After many years of practice and a promising future, she went back to school to receive a Masters in Organizational Communications. Her thesis was on delivery of dental care. Laurie is going to develop materials that are useful to the indigent patient using simple graphics to explain dental prevention. The materials will be printed in English and Spanish.

What a sacrifice Laurie has made to help a group of people who may never know her but will reap the benefits of her work. Yet, Laurie does not see it as a sacrifice. "Working with the indigent has opened my eyes to the rest of the world and has given me the energy to get involved," she said. "Caring for people has become a vital part of my life and has been so gratifying. I also learned to back up a 34-foot van using only the mirrors!" Laurie has learned that purpose comes from helping others.

* * * * *

It is never too late to get involved. Dr. Warren Schafer was nearing the end of a long and productive practice in dentistry ten years ago. He got his start in dentistry during World War II as a Navy corpsman helping the dentist. After the war, he went to dental school and later started his practice. As a Christian, he felt a desire to help others. He began doing community service helping out as a volunteer fireman, volunteering with the Oregon Department of Fish and Wildlife, and providing free dental care for battered women in the county shelter. In 1988, Dr. Shafer picked up some material about our mission. As he read the mission statement, a phrase caught his attention, "—to demonstrate the love of Christ to those in crisis..." As a Christian doctor, he wanted to see if the mission was genuine. After asking questions and seeing the work we do, he believed in our mission. He volunteered one day a month in the mobile dental unit.

In 1994, Dr. Schafer sold his practice. Instead of involving himself in recreation, Dr. Schafer began a new life of "pure dentistry" — dentistry without all the management problems. He volunteered nine or more days a month on the mobile van, and spent much time requesting the state government to give malpratice relief to doctors so more would volunteer. Jennie, his wife, is always with him, and helps him in all of his endeavors. The couple went to Uzbekstan, a former Russian Republic, for our mission and stayed eighteen days performing dentistry.

I read an article written by Dr. Schafer where he described his feelings about doing this work. "I am enjoying every minute. I am doing dentistry without a care for management. I am doing what I was trained to do. For my salary, I receive thanks, hand shakes, hugs and kisses. I smell the roses all the way."

It is volunteers like Dr. Warren and Jennie who help us provide so much care here and around the world with so little money. For years, we have been able to maintain an average of 97% of donations going directly to the programs we have. The 1993 issue of Money Magazine had an article entitled, "The Best Charities in America," listing NWMT as the third best health charity in America! That year, 97.1% of donations went directly to helping people. Our staff worked hard to maintain a low overhead, but volunteers who gave their time also made it possible.

In 1991, President George Bush awarded NWMT the 403rd "Daily Point of Light" award for the work of that first mobile unit. In his letter to us, he said: "We must not allow ourselves to be measured by the sum of our possessions or the size of our bank accounts. The true measure of any individual is found in the way he or she treats others - — and the person who regards others with love, respect, and charity holds a priceless treasure in his heart. With that in mind, I have often noted that, from now on in America, any definition of a successful life must include serving others. Your efforts provide a shining example of this standard."

Dr. Lee Emery, Laurie Johnson, Dr. Warren and Jennie Schafer and hundreds of others have certainly found what a successful and meaningful life brings when one gives of himself to help another.

* * * * *

Dave Farqhar came to the mission back in 1988 when Jean

hired him to help with our banquets. I saw something very special in this young man. He possessed a lot of energy, creativity and leadership qualities.

About this same time, I noticed how many countries in the world lacked basic medical equipment and supplies. With the good name we had developed, I thought that factories, hospitals and other suppliers might be willing to donate medical supplies and equipment to us for distribution.

I asked Dave if he would like to take on the challenge of making the vision a reality. Dave put his heart into developing this program. Armed with an idea, Dave developed a distribution center that now sends out over $60 million dollars a year of medicines, medical equipment, food and other commodities to countries everywhere including our own. It has become the largest distribution center of its kind on the west coast.

Dave gathered a few people to help him who were his keys to the center being a success. A couple by the name of Fred and Ruth Boruck were past retirement age, but had no intention of settling down. Desiring a meaningful retirement, they started volunteering. Soon, they were using their skills to help Dave grow the procurement and distribution program. They continued working for many years, demonstrating how to use lifetime skills for others.

They were two very different personalities. Ruth was driven to accomplish her goals, yet she had a soft and gentle heart. When she saw a suffering child, the tears would come. Fred was quiet and gentle. He had a twinkle in his eye that made you want to do anything for him. Fred was my personal encourager. When the pressures of my work would mount up, Fred seemed to know it was time to say words like, "Ron, don't be discouraged. You are doing a wonderful job. God is pleased with you."

These two precious people helped gather millions of donated supplies for needy people. Finally, while in their seventies, we asked them to come on staff and what a job they have done! One example of their accomplishments was that Fred procured five million dollars worth of donated seeds. These seeds have now provided enough food to feed millions of poor people in the former

Russian Republics, in Africa and in southeast Asia. The crops these seeds provided will feed hungry people for a long time.

While Fred and Ruth and others were busy procuring these medicines and food supplies, we attempted to solve a difficult challenge in the warehouse. Most of the supplies came to us disorganized. The boxes began to stack up. In answer to our prayers, Wanetah "Jo" Bell walked into our lives. After reading about our mission and hearing of our need for volunteers, Jo answered the call. She organized our sorting area, and established inventory procedures for packaging like-kind medical supplies. She developed a system for getting the boxes shipped to their destinations undamaged.

For over six years, Jo came into the distribution center and worked four to five days a week! One time, I asked Jo why she gave so much time. She said, "I worked for a living for many years, but now I have found something that has given me purpose."

On August 27, 1998, a heart attack took Fred Boruck away to be with God. One week later on September 3, 1998, cancer took Jo Bell from us, too. While Jo Bell was nearing death and I visited her, she would say, "Oh, Ron, I want to come back and work in the distribution center so bad!" Shortly before Jo passed away, she wrote Jean and me a letter.

Dear Ron and Jean,

Bless you for giving me the chance to serve my God and fellow man in such a rewarding way by sorting and packing for Northwest Medical Teams. When I re-read my Northwest Medical Teams Presidential Citation that hangs on my living room wall, I am so proud to have been one who did serve you well! Please continue the good work and I'll try to look after you and your "project" from "up there." Have a great day and do the best job yet in helping others.
My love and blessings,

Jo Bell

Millions of people have better lives today because of Fred and Jo. I know they would want these two things: that life-changing medical supplies and foods continue to be shipped to the neediest areas, and that someone step into their places of service.

Many people have faithfully volunteered year after year in our headquarters office and distribution center. Though I wish I could name every one of them, the list would be too long. Carol Pauly Bliem and Millie Boldman have served over five years; Donna Pierce over seven years; Tom Jones over eight years; and Warren and Anne Craig have served faithfully over nine years! All of these people spent years working in their professions and now give their time to serve others. They and many more like them have helped to get those precious commodities out of the distribution center and at the same time it has brought great meaning to their own lives. The world is better off today because of Fred Boruck, Jo Bell, and all these people ... and God is well pleased.

Floods In Our Backyard

Flooding is one of the most destructive forces. After witnessing small floods, I saw the damage caused by water. However, in the mid-nineties, I was stunned by seeing the destruction caused by flooding in the mid-west and southern states. We responded with work teams around the St. Louis, Missouri area when the waters of the Mississippi river overflowed its banks as well as did its tributaries. Boating down the streets of Newton, Georgia, where the water nearly covered the downtown buildings, I realized the heartbreak of losing one's home.

Unsuspectedly, the mid-west and southern states floods helped to prepare our teams for a flood in our own back yard. In 1996, many areas in western Oregon became flooded when rivers overflowed. God prepared us for the tragedy. We had just been given 20,000 blankets to distribute. We had never received that many in our history. We had also just received 40,000 pounds of canned food and all this was on our shelves in the distribution center when the flood occurred.

We immediately contacted the media to let them know we needed volunteers in our distribution center to pack family boxes for distribution and that we also needed volunteers to go out and help families. The response was tremendous. Hundreds of people came forward to help and thousands began sending money. Before long, we had raised a million dollars in cash and a million dollars in supplies for flood victims.

Our staff could not possibly handle the task of distributing all of the supplies or organizing the volunteer teams to help the devastated families of the flood. It was thrilling to see the number of key people who came forward to volunteer. For example, Dick Roland had retired from an executive job. He was still in his fifties and wanted to do something with his life that would be of service to the Lord. After observing him at work, Dick was asked to coordinate the flood effort.

Dick accepted the challenge. He set up charts so he could know where all of the teams were. He organized delivery trips for trucks to haul supplies to the small towns that were flooded. He coordinated our efforts with those of city and county officials, as well as the Salvation Army and Red Cross.

NWMT had accumulated over a million dollars to help the flood victims. After the flood waters subsided, Dick went into another phase of the outreach. Small grants were given to people who had no insurance and were on low incomes so they could buy materials for rebuilding. Over two hundred families were helped back into their homes through these grants.

Dick caught the vision of the power of one person. Rather than settling into retirement, he decided to make a difference. He realized that the knowledge he had gathered in the work place was valued and could be used by God. Dick represents many others who are the success of this mission.

Family Testimonies

The first short term medical trip Dr. Dan McDougal made with our mission was in 1986 to Mexico. After responding with a medical team in the aftermath of the earthquake, we had returned to help those who were homeless as a result. Dr. Dan helped us establish a medical clinic in a very poor area of Mexico City. After staying a month, Dan was moved by his experiences. Believing God wanted him to do more, he and his wife Lindsey started doing short term mission trips around the world.

They moved their family to West Africa for nearly a year to care for people. Dr. Dan told me that each time they worked together on a short mission, they found their sharing and relationship was different from any they could have experienced at home, either personally or professionally.

Dan said, "Throughout the month of work in Somalia, Lindsey and I experienced together the joy of serving, the fatigue and physical discomfort of the land and work, and the stress related to the limited resources and diversity of the team. However, all those things, when seen in retrospect, were relationship growing and strengthening events. We have shared an experience few married couples can have. We also have found that our good memories far outweigh those related to the grief of lost people and tragedy. The Somalia experience was more eventful and emotion- packed than all the previous trips. We found ourselves, on a daily basis, looking to each other for strength and encouragement. We shared an emotional bond that possibly only those who are married could appreciate."

Dr. Dan and Dr. Lindsey have been a model for their children. Their twelve-year-old daughter has served as a full team member in the jungles of Peru working alongside her parents. The McDougal's are raising their children to send them out into the world with values and a sense of what a meaningful life is.

Working with Dan and Lindsey and seeing the other couples working together have shown me how helping others can bring families closer. It forms a bond as nothing else can. I have even seen how parents and their children are drawn closer through the parents going to help others. I think about the Cavens' children encouraging Dr. Phyllis and Dr. Travis to go back in 1979 or Shari Pfeiffer's children who encouraged her to go.

Shari and others have told me how much the experience drew their family together.

Marie Davis is a nurse who has gone to far off places many times to help save lives. She and her husband, Curt, have worked together on many trips. Curt is an electrician who is willing to use his talents, or do what is needed, such as go to an Indian Village to dig trenches for clean water lines to be laid. This couple took their two small children, Rachel and Jennifer, to Sudan, and the experience made a profound change in their family. It helped set values and priorities for all of them. Jennifer became a nurse like her mom so she could help people.

Bob Hamlin is one of our board members from Boise, Idaho. He and his wife, Carol, went on a team to Mexico to help distribute food packages to poor people. Bob told me what an impact it made on him to watch Carol interact with the poor children. He said it was a tremendous bonding time between them as they worked together to offer hope and love to the poorest of the poor. Bob said, "We have taken many vacation trips over the years we have been married, but this trip was, without doubt, the most meaningful trip we have ever taken. We will never be the same again."

Another man told me how troubled he had become as a father. He did well financially, and was able to provide everything his family needed. However, his children's attitudes troubled him. Unsatisfied, they did not appreciate the things they had. The father grew up with little and had appreciated what he received. He hoped to bring his children back to reality.

He heard about the work of Northwest Medical Teams in Mexico and wondered if he could take his whole family on a work project there. When he called our headquarters, he found there was a project he could take them on which involved working with the dump people in Mexico City. When he broached the subject of the trip with his family, they initially said, "No way!" He continued to bring the subject up until they agreed to go. They were not excited about the trip.

When they walked into the dump, they were shocked. They cried for a long period after leaving the first day. Each day the family worked, they got to know the people more and fell in love with them. What they marveled at was, in spite of their unbelievable poverty, the children of the dump seemed so happy. When they gave some small thing to them or the adults, they were so appreciative. The children confessed to the father that, had they been given the same, it would have meant nothing to them. The father said the trip brought his family closer than they had ever been and each of them was impacted. They returned with different priorities and a desire to do what they could to continue helping.

We help our children by demonstrating the importance of helping others. Families who care together are strengthened. These people have certainly helped to bring the family of Northwest Medical Teams together.

Each individual and family I have shared about in this chapter have run or are running the course set out for them just as I believe God has a course for each of us to run. Getting on the course leads to meaning and purpose for our lives. My life has been enriched by knowing and working with so many people who have demonstrated what caring is all about. My own course in life was found by bringing people together to run the course of "good works."

Nurse Marie Davis, left, helping an Albanian during the 1999 crisis in Kosovo. Marie Davis has been out on 29 teams since being on the first team in 1984 during the Ethiopian famine. No other volunteer has come close to her record. Photo courtesy of Marie Davis.

CHAPTER TWELVE

CATCH A TRAIN

Let us hold unswervingly to the hope we profess, for he who promised is faithful. And let us consider how we may spur one another on toward love and good deeds. Hebrews 10:23,24

Northwest Medical Teams is a train whose tracks lead to places where people need help. An empty train is no good to anyone. Only when the train is loaded with people willing to help does NWMT make a difference. There are many stations for the train to stop and many opportunities for people to help make a difference in someone's life.

The conductor is calling all those who can hear to get on board. The train is never full. There is always room for more. The cost to ride is a willing heart. The ride is not always comfortable, but the experience is always rewarding, meaningful, and satisfying.

Northwest Medical Teams is not the only train of its kind. Other trains include local churches, civic clubs, schools, and other non-profit organizations. Trains are available in many places, and riding one helps us discover what we may have been missing out on a sense of meaning and purpose.

Before hopping on one of these trains of compassion, a person might want to think about a few questions before climbing aboard.

Where is my destination? My 93-year-old father awoke one morning in October 1998, and discovered he could not move his arms and legs. He called my brother, Carl, and told him he thought his mind was going. He had probably suffered a stroke.

Carl and my brother, Wiley, went to his house and made him comfortable. Later, Carl called me to say that Papa was near death; he probably would not make it through the night. Because my father lived in San Juan Capistrano, California, I would not reach him in time.

Carl said that they had a wonderful day together. He said they talked about the old days, shared their love for one another, and talked about what to do with things after he was gone. It was a very special time for all of them.

About 8 p.m., I called Papa. "I understand you are not doing very well, Papa."

The frail voice on the other end of the phone answered, "No, I am not, Son." He continued, "I was praying this morning, and I asked God to let me go be with Mama. Then, I saw Mama standing at a door waiting for me!"

My heart leaped. I said, "Oh Papa, do you know what this means? The Lord is about to do something wonderful for you." I told him that I would pray that his prayer be answered that evening. We shared our love for one another, and how much we would miss each other.

The last thing he said was, "Son, I will be waiting for you." I hung up and prayed. God is so good. One hour later, Papa closed his eyes and went to sleep. Today, he is with Mama and all the loved ones who chose to follow Christ.

Though I do not know my future, I hope my ending is like Papa's. On his last day Papa was able to share his love with nearly all his children and receive ours in return. Knowing I have the love of my wife, my children, my grandchildren and the many friends I have is so important to me. Yet, still more important is knowing my destination. Is it heaven? We should all ask this question.

If heaven is my destination then I need to care for the same things God cares for. The most important thing to God beyond my relationship with Jesus Christ, are his people. Therefore he wants me to help care for them. And when I'm involved in these "good works" the Bible says I am storing up riches in heaven while discovering meaning and purpose in this present life. Therefore, my train destination is wherever people need help.

What kind of eternal legacy do I wish to leave? Before beginning NWMT, I wrestled with this question for many years. Though I knew how I wanted to spend my last minutes, I was unsure of how my loved ones would remember me.

I thought about all my activities and accomplishments of which I was proud: my successful business ventures, my singing days in both rock and roll and gospel, my love of fishing and vegetable gardening, and my appearances on the news for NWMT. These were all good aspects of who I was, yet the question continued to nag at me.

Several years after starting this mission, I had lunch with a friend. While telling him a story about the work of our medical teams in Ethiopia, he stopped me and said, "Ron, what a wonderful legacy you are leaving for your family and all of us who know you."

I paused and responded, "I had not thought about that before."

Then, my friend said something I will never forget. "Having the opportunity of wealth, yet devoting your life to help others is about the best legacy one could leave behind." The words sunk deeply into my heart.

I told him I appreciated what he said. I am content in this line of work. I have not felt as much peace in doing anything else. I would not give up all the memories of seeing children brought back from the brink of death for all the riches I could have amassed.

Legacies do not always appear the same. Yet, eternal legacies have one common aspect — service to others. My brother, Carl, and his wife, Cheri, have a successful business. They used their wealth to start a non-profit Drug Education and Rehabilitation Program called "Brandy's Friends" in Laguna Beach, California. They completely financed the operation for years and even now contribute the vast majority of support. This program has helped hundreds of young people to either get off drugs or avoid starting. Their lives exemplify true success and their work shows genuine wealth (heavenly riches).

Dale and Gail are friends of mine who have used their wealth in a variety of ways as a service to others. Both of them grew up without a lot of money, but were taught the eternal principles about giving. Dale had a creative idea for a business, and the idea turned out to be a financial boom for him and Gail. They saw the success as an opportunity to give back to God for all the blessings in their life. Just as they had learned to give, they wanted their three children to grow up understanding what giving and serving is. With their money, they have significantly helped not only NWMT, but many other missions and charities, by giving away more than 50% of their income. Their goal is to give most of their wealth away so it will serve God.

On the other hand, Dale's brother, Dave, was called to full-time Christian ministry. He and his family has served as missionaries in Africa for fifteen years. Now he is overseeing all mission works for his denomination. Both of these brothers are being the hands of God in different ways, but both are leaving an eternal legacy for their family and friends.

Another friend, Conrad Pearson started a small business of advising people in good, financial planning. The effort grew into a very large business with many associates and other employees. He and his wife, Barb, involved themselves in the community by helping a women's shelter and a mental health facility. They also organized a community coalition of churches. Conrad participated in Rotary Club and the Chamber of Commerce, serving as president of both. They also began a foundation to serve the city's needs. Both Conrad and Barb were chosen "Citizens of the Year" for the community.

All of these people will be remembered for a life of giving! They use their resources and time to make someone else's life better. I doubt children and friends will talk about business successes after these people die. Instead, they will reminisce about how generous and kind they were.

What does it cost? The rich, the middle class, and poor will always be among us. Class distinctions began for Israel when they begged for a king, rather than God, to lead them (I Samuel

8). God warned them about the consequences. The king would draft young men into his army. He would take their daughters and make them cooks and bakers for him and his elite. He would take the best of the crops, a tenth of their grain, flocks, and wine to give to his elite. He would then enslave the people. God warned Israel that people would cry out for relief from the king, but the Lord would not answer. When I read this, I realized that very little has changed.

However, the fact of class distinctions does not eliminate our responsibility to the poor. God gave specific instructions to Israel about the rich helping those less fortunate. His concern for the poor was great, and he expected those with enough to give to those without enough. The Bible is full of commands to give to the poor. In the book of Proverbs alone, the instructions given for the sake of the poor are many.

Wise Solomon wrote:

"He who oppresses the poor shows contempt for their Maker, but whoever is kind to the needy honors God."(Proverbs 14:31)

"He who is kind to the poor lends to the Lord, and he will reward him for what he has done."(Proverbs 19:17)

"If a man shuts his ears to the cry of the poor, he too will cry out and not be answered."(Proverbs 21:13)

"A generous man will himself be blessed, for he shares his food with the poor."(Proverbs 22:9) "

He who gives to the poor will lack nothing, but he who closes his eyes to them receives many curses."(Proverbs 28:27)

"Speak up and judge fairly; defend the rights of the poor and needy."(Proverbs 31:9)

"Rich and poor have this in common: The Lord is the Maker of them all." (Proverbs 22:2)

However, the rich of Israel did not take this to heart and they did not care for the poor. They built their big homes far away from the poor and would not enter the poor neighborhoods. God reminded Israel how much He would bless them if they followed His instructions. However, they did not listen. Instead, they worshipped idols and false gods, and the rich continued to treat the poor with disdain.

"And the word of the Lord came again to Zechariah: 'This is what the Lord Almighty says: 'Administer true justice; show mercy and compassion to one another. Do not oppress the widow or the fatherless, the alien or the poor. In your hearts do not think evil of each other.' "But they refused to pay attention; stubbornly they turned their backs and stopped up their ears. They made their hearts as hard as flint and would not listen to the law or to the words that the Lord Almighty had sent by his Spirit through the earlier prophets. So the Lord Almighty was very angry." Zechariah 7:8-14. Then the Lord said that Israel would be scattered among all the nations, where they would be strangers. Israel would not be a nation again for over two thousand years.

After reading the Bible and many books written by Biblical scholars, I learned that class distinction will always be here until God changes it one day through His Son. Is it wrong to be rich? No, I think not. However, with wealth comes responsibility for the poor.

Sharing one's riches blesses both receiver and giver. Giving brings meaning and purpose to lives. I shared the example of Dale and Gail, the young couple who gives more than 50% of their wealth to help others. They still have enough left to care for their family and for their days when Dale can no longer work, but their plan is to give almost all of it away that it may bless others. What more do they need? They have truly found meaning and purpose for their lives.

It would be very difficult for most of us to give 50% of our earnings away. However, witnessing what Dale and Gail do encourages me to think about my priorities. I stop to ask myself the question, "Do I really need to buy that?" I have found myself able to give more of my resources just by thinking about what is eternally important.

For example, I used to enjoy trading in for a new car every year or so, which would cost me several thousand dollars. Now, these facts often stop me. Several thousand dollars could provide surgery for fifteen elderly Indians in Mexico who are blind because of cataracts. Fifteen people could see again! Fifteen children with cleft lip and palates could have a chance for a normal life. Several thousand dollars could provide a nutritious breakfast and education classes for a year to six impoverished children living in the dump of Mexico City.

When I think about these possibilities, it keeps me focused on the priority I believe God would have me follow. After all, Jesus said the greatest commandment or priorities for my life are to love the Lord my God with all my heart and with all my soul and with all my mind and to love my neighbor as I would want them to love me. (Matthew 22:37-40 paraphrased) If I were hungry, sick, homeless, or distressed, I would hope someone would help me.

It is not only the wealthy that can find meaning and purpose in giving. Everyone can find it through sacrifice, whether it is money or time. When I read a letter scribbled from an obvious widow who encloses $15 and apologizes because she lives on $700 a month and can not give more, the tears still come. My house payment is more than she is living on! Yet, she can find a way to send $15 to help someone else. A recent study has found that the poor give a greater percentage of their income than the middle or upper class. It humbles me to think about people who sacrifice for a cause.

Having financial security and retirement are worthy goals, but if they were my only goals, my life would still be empty. Something would have been missing. Having a life of meaning and purpose gives me the ultimate satisfaction in life. It will cost us time and perhaps personal resources but climbing aboard a train of compassion creates a beautiful legacy.

Why should I get on board? If the answer to this question is that you have been programmed to "catch a train," most of us would say, "NO WAY." A person likes to think he is his own person. Ephesians 2:10 reads, "For we are God's workmanship, created in Christ Jesus to do good works, which God prepared in advance for us to do." I thought about that. It says "we." Every human being is God's workmanship. Every one of us was created in Christ Jesus to do good works and God prepared every one of us from the very beginning for that purpose. Does that mean I was programmed by God? Is that why I feel so good when I am serving others?

I was reminded of how elated volunteers feel after returning from a volunteer trip. Though they went to help others, the volunteers returned feeling they had been receivers. They felt great! It has little to do with people's belief in God — both Christians and non-Christians alike feel similarly after involving themselves with helping others or doing "good works." God created all people and programmed them all the same. Many have not discovered that they were programmed by the Creator.

The verse in Ephesians means something special to this generation — the age of computers. Computer programs are written by people and placed into computers. Likewise, God wrote a program and put it into us. What a wonderful feeling to discover that truth. He programmed all of us to reach out to other people.

God reached out to the world when He took the form of man, Jesus. My acceptance of Jesus Christ ministered to me. My reaching out to others also ministers to me because I am doing what I was created to do. There is something in it for me when I follow Him. I am promised eternal life. There is something in it for me when I do good works for others. The prize is not worldly success, money, nor retirement, but it's the inner peace and joy I receive because I am doing what I was created to do.

Reader's Digest once reported a scientific study performed on two groups of people. One group gave of their time and treasure to charity. The other group did not. After ten years, the study indicated that the group who gave their time and treasure to charity seemed to live longer and healthier lives than those who did not. God created us to do "good works," and when we are doing what we were programmed to do, we are happier people. Being happy promotes longer and healthier lives.

Getting on my train can make you a happier, more contented, and healthier person. That is why I like riding this train and that is why I am always inviting more to get on board. Riding this train lets me live out what I was created to do.

When is the right time? God called me to this ministry, but if I had not acted on it, the things we have done would never have happened, or it would have happened to someone else. Now is the time to get on the train. I heard a story about a bishop who had forgotten his watch. He asked his traveling companion, Mother Teresa, what time it was. When asked the question, Mother Teresa, who did not own a watch or much of anything, simply replied, "The time is now!" If we have been programmed by God to do "good works," then now is the time to begin.

A scetch performed by Phil Nash, a Christian drama actor, explains the importance of acting now. Here are the scenes that Phil acted out in his drama:

Scene One: A young boy has a baseball mitt on and is throwing a ball up and catching it. The boy speaks to God. "Lord, I saw all those starving children on television last night. That was terrible. I wish I could help them. When I get older, I want you to use me to help those people. Use me, Lord."

Scene Two: The young boy is in college. He speaks to God. "Lord, I want to thank you for the baseball scholarship you helped me get. By the way, Lord, remember how I wanted to help the poor? Well, as soon as I finish college, I want you to use me, Lord. Use me, Lord."

Scene Three: The young man is now married. He speaks to God. "Lord, thank you for getting me through college and now for the wonderful family you gave me. I am so blessed. Thank you for the new business I have. Oh, by the way, Lord, I have not forgotten about wanting to help the poor. But, you know, Lord, I got this business to run and I need to save money for the children's college. As soon as that is done, I will be ready. I want you to use me, Lord. Use me, Lord."

Scene Four: The man is now very old and near death. He speaks to God. "Lord, I feel so lonely. I really miss my wife since she passed away. I miss the children, also. They don't seem to come around much. By the way, Lord, remember how I wanted you to use me.? Why didn't you use me, Lord? Why didn't you use me?"

I turned 61 years old in 1999. Time has flown. If you are young, you think you have forever. If you are forty, you know what I mean. Life slips by so fast. It is easy to get caught up in the game of life and forget what is important. There is a quote that reads, "Life is like a coin. You can spend it any way you choose, but you can only spend it once." I want to be sure I am spending my coin wisely. If you feel you have not been spending it as wisely as you should, it is never too late to change.

Many senior citizens are involved with NWMT, and they are such a blessing. Some come to our distribution center to help package medical supplies; others volunteer to make calls from their homes.

There are many examples of people who did not believe they were too old to give. The Order of the Eastern Star of the Northwest decided to make Northwest Medical Teams their charity project for 1998. They knew we needed toys for our children's "Gift Of Hope" Christmas boxes we hand out to poor children in the United States, Mexico, Romania and Moldova. We distribute over 16,000 boxes every year. They also wanted to make Afghan baby blankets for our orphans of Romania. One of the members, a 94-year-old lady, told her friends that she would like to make an Afghan blanket, but she was not sure she would finish it before she died. The wonderful lady completed not one, but five blankets! Then, she asked, "Now what can I do?"

Ansgar, a dear friend of mine, is still working to serve his neighbor in his later years. Though he is still involved with his car dealership in Woodland, Washington, he now serves as an elder in his local Presbyterian Church and helps them with projects. For eight years, Ansgar also has organized a fundraising banquet for our mission. After living in Woodland for over 80 years, he has accumulated a large group of friends. People find it hard to say "no" to the Norwegian. He persuades his friends to sponsor a table, and fill it with people. Each year, approximately 250 people come out to this small town of a few thousand people. During these years, the banquets have raised well over $200,000! Ansgar loves doing this because he knows the hours he spends helping get people to a banquet will result in many lives being helped.

After a career in the United States Navy, Richard discovered he had multiple sclerosis. Eventually, he lost the use of all his body except for his head. Richard lives in a nursing home and is restricted to either his bed or an electric wheelchair. I got to know Richard years ago after he had sent a gift to our mission, and I visited him when I heard he was in a nursing home. I learned to love this man for his strength and sense of humor.

Richard has a deep faith in Christ. He listens to the Catholic radio station in Portland, Oregon, faithfully. The attendants wake him at midnight for Mass. He is able to turn the pages of his big print Bible, which he reads faithfully. He also spends much time in prayer. Though Richard cannot go out and build a health center in Mexico or fix up an orphanage in Romania, he can still ride our train of hope. Why? Because he has a willing heart. He supports it financially, so others can build, fix, and heal. Though he is not wealthy according to the world's standards, he gives what he can to help. He also participates by praying for our work and for the people we serve.

The time is now! Some say they have to wait to board the train until they are out of school, money is saved, children are older, or business is better. Some do not board because they feel they are not skilled or talented enough. The excuses sound valid, but they are still excuses. The joy of riding the train will pass them by. It's fun! It's rewarding! It's life-changing! Isn't that what all of us have wanted all along? We do not have to wait to do what we were created to do. The time is now!

Am I willing to ride with others?

I love football! When I have time, I enjoy watching a game on Sunday afternoon. When I was a young boy and all we had was radio, I loved to hear the great athlete and sportscaster Tom Harmon. He told wonderful stories of the feats of the great athletes. One football player about whom I loved to hear stories was called "the galloping ghost," Red Grange of Illinois. With a nickname like that, a young boy's heart would beat quicker at the sound of it. Tom told how Red made history on October 18, 1924, against Michigan. No other player has ever had a day like his.

The first time Red got the ball, he ran 95 yards for a touchdown. The second time, he ran 67 yards for a touchdown. The third time he got the ball, he ran 56 yards for a touchdown. And... the fourth time he got the ball, he ran 44 yards for, you guessed it, a touchdown. He had the ball four times, scored four times, covered 262 yards, and still had not been stopped or tackled!

That was an amazing feat. Though Red Grange got the applause and his name went into the record book, Red did not perform the amazing feat alone. Illinois had a great football team with players in front of Red knocking opposing players out of the way so Red could make those great runs.

The workings of a team are similar when one climbs on this train. You are never alone. Your teammates help all the way. Whether the train is Northwest Medical Teams, a civic club, a school, the battered women's shelter, a homeless shelter, the food bank, the children's hospital, the meals on wheels, the senior center, or your church, there will always be other teammates.

I love living in the Northwest. I know there are other great places to live in this wonderful nation, but I am partial to Oregon. A great experience is to wake up to the sound of Canadian geese flying overhead. Sometimes, I will run outside to catch a glimpse of the majestic creatures as they soar above me in a "V" formation.

Researchers have learned that the "V" flight pattern creates a draft. Each one can fly in the draft of the other, and thereby reduce its stress. When the leader grows weary, he drops to the rear and another will take his place. This method of flying in formation is so efficient, the geese can actually fly 71% farther as a group than they ever could on their own. Another team aspect researchers have discovered is that when one goose gets in trouble and lands, several others land too. They stay with it until it gets better or dies.

Geese were designed by God to function as a team, one depending on the other. Likewise, the Lord has designed us to work together. Geese are simply following their instincts. We, however, are given a choice. It is sad that many people try to go it alone, and find it hard to be team players.

Tony Campolo, the well-known university professor, author, humanitarian, and Christian speaker, once told a story about a wealthy man who had one last desire. When he died, his desire was to be buried sitting upright in his Cadillac with a cigar in his mouth in the "Cemetery of the Stars," known as Forest Lawn in Southern California.

The undertakers dug a big hole and lowered the Cadillac with the deceased man propped upright, cigar in his mouth. As the car was lowered, one of the undertakers was heard saying, "Man...that's really living." When I heard Tony tell this story I laughed with everyone else. What a funny thing to say! Then I thought about it.

Imagine what small plots cost in a place like Forest Lawn, let alone one big enough to accommodate a Cadillac! I believe this man must have cared only for himself and his own selfish desires. He was not a team player. Hungry children could have benefited from the cost of the big plot and the sale of the Cadillac. Instead of making his life count with meaning and purpose, the best he could get was a, "Man, that's really living?" from the undertaker. Such a life is not living, but dying. This poor soul had to have been dying for most of his life.

Team work has been defined as, "The fuel that allows common people to attain uncommon results." Teams of common people attaining unbelievable results here and around the world have been the stuff of my life's work. The lame walk, the blind see, the poor are fed, the orphan is cared for, the sick are healed, and the hopeless lifted up. I have shared in the joy these teams get in these accomplishments. I have never seen people stand higher or feel more self worth than when they are on the train bound for mercy. Mercy is a place where the receiver and the giver blend into one.

Live!

Dear children, let us not love with words or tongue but with actions and in truth. I John 3:18

Life that is not lived as God created it to be, is not real living! Actions do speak louder than words.

Barbara De Angeles wrote a book entitled *Real Moments.* In it she wrote:

"First I was dying to finish high school and start college; and then I was dying to finish college and start working; and then I was dying for my children to grow old enough for school, so I could return to work; and then I was dying to retire...and now, I am dying...and suddenly I realize I forgot to live!"

It is a tragedy that so many of us will come to the end of our lives only to discover that we have not really lived. The time sthat we allowed God to truly use us we could count on one hand. Have you ever wondered how God could use you? Perhaps you have had moments when you felt God wanted you to do something but you did not know how or where to begin. First let me encourage you by saying I have felt insufficient and wondered how God could use me at times in my life but yet look how God used me through founding Northwest Medical Teams International.

Second, if you want to know how or where to begin, let me encourage you to do what I did. If you do, I am convinced you will get those questions answered. I sum it up this way:

1. I chose to "Love the Lord my God with all of my heart, mind and soul." I made Him first in my life. I sought His face all along the way. He never disappointed me once. At times I have been disappointed by people but never by Him. By making Him first I had to give Him ownership and control over everything. That was a conscious decision on my part. God could not be in first place if I had taken ownership and control. I would have failed. When I was able to truly give Him ownership and control, the burden was off me and I was able to see His hand in each step as we grew which allowed us to reach out to more and more people.

2. I wanted to obey the last part of God's number one commandment to "Love my neighbor as myself." To do that, I had to establish who was my closest neighbor. The closest neighbor to me was Jean and my children. God did not say my job was the priority but my neighbor was my priority. That has been a tough one for me and if you are an "A" type personality, you know what I mean. If I am not careful, it would be easy to let my job be not only ahead

of my neighbor in priority but could even be ahead of my priority to love my God first. Every time I have allowed my job to be a higher priority, I have found myself in trouble. God does not care about my position, my bank account, my house or my car even though He provides these nice things for us. He cares about relationships. They are the most important.

3. I had to get help from others in order to maintain the first and second priority for my life. When I wanted to form Northwest Medical Teams Intl as a permanent mission, Doug Coe told me to go back to Oregon and form a focus group that would hold me accountable for God's priorities for my life. I met with that group for seven months before I understood what God wanted me to do. Out of group is where we found the "how and where to begin." I continue to this day meeting every Friday with a group of men at noon. We pray for each other, for our families, for how we can be better husbands and we remind ourselves of the need to keep God first in our lives.

4. I had to ask for help. I would never have succeeded without asking people for help. I found people ready and willing to help and that made my job easier. I found we could do far more as a team than I could ever do as an individual. Teamwork is the most powerful tool God uses on earth. He works through His people and He loves it when we work as a team. The bible says, "We have not because we ask not." I found scripture after scripture of God telling us to let people know the needs of the poor and to ask for their help. This mission has succeeded because we followed God's command to "ask." People are ready to give of their time and treasure to the right cause.

5. I had to be accountable to God and man. God will always hold us accountable for our deeds but we must also be accountable to man. To do this, I made sure we did everything at arm's length so that we could always account for everything we did. I made sure we had an independent auditor come in every year and scrutinize our books and system and then publish that report. I made sure

that everyone including myself was never overpaid. The ministries I have seen get in trouble were those that would not be accountable to God and to man.

You may not feel led to begin a ministry like Northwest Medical Teams but it doesn't matter what you are led to do. If you follow the points I have summed up, you will succeed in this life and in what you do. I promise!

It took me many years to discover that living is more than going to school, getting a job, raising a family, and enjoying material things. It has been said, "We make a living by what we do, but we make a life by what we do for others." Once I was ready to step out of my comfort zone, God allowed me to see the opportunities that awaited me. Miracles were in my future. Without that step of faith, I would not have witnessed Fredrico see again, Ramon have his cleft lip and palate corrected, Oscar have his rotten teeth repaired, or children receive a gift of hope in a Christmas box. I would never have seen these wonderful teams of volunteers turn hopelessness into hope.

The train is puffing and smoking, ready to move down the tracks. Seats are empty, waiting to be filled. The conductor is calling, "All aboard!" Will you climb on board?

Soon I will be retiring from the ministry of Northwest Medical Teams Intl to begin enjoying some time with my family and in particular with Kai, Halle, Sarah, and Hope my wonderful and fun grandchildren. I wanted to be a grandfather for years and now I know how wonderful it is. The joy they bring to Jean and me is beyond words.

I use the word retire very looocly because I am not really retired and never will be as long as the Lord allows me to work. I have not found retirement in the bible yet. I really believe God has a purpose for us until the day we close our eyes for the last time. One gift God has allowed me to have is a gift in building up the resources be it people or funding to accomplish the mission. God used this gift to build Northwest Medical Teams Intl into the mission it is today. So in having this gift, I decided I could multiply myself by helping not only Northwest Medical Teams Intl but also other worthy missions to grow their resources.

For years while leading and helping Northwest Medical Teams grow, I became aware of many other missions. Many of them struggle with finding enough resources to do the good works. They lack the training in developing the needed resources. There are few places to get the necessary training. Being someone who enjoys seeing God's work grows, I decided I could be of perhaps greater help by helping many missions and thereby multiply myself. I have watched Northwest Medical Teams Intl grow from birth to a wonderful mission accomplishing $80 million dollars a year of work here and around the world. Now I want to take what God has taught me through these years and give it away to other missions so they can grow.

Thanks to the support of a friend, I have begun working with a number of missions. I am acting as an unpaid consultant to these missions who cannot afford one but I do have criteria for helping them. They must be missions who truly have a good vision for helping people, they must be accountable to God and to man, and they must have a strong desire to learn. It has already proven to be a wonderful experience as I work with these missions and see the excitement it is generating. When I see them gain in their resource development and they share with me how much it will mean to their work, I find I receive the same joy as if I was still at Northwest Medical Teams where my heart will always be.

I still stand amazed after these twenty years of being with Northwest Medical Teams Intl that God would have used me in such a wonderful way. I am amazed because you see in the way the present world measures the qualifications to do such a thing; I should never have been able to accomplish this. If I had been someone applying for the position of President of Northwest Medical Teams Intl years ago, my application and resume would not have even been considered. Even though I have received two honorary doctorate degrees since being the Founder and President, I do not have an earned degree!

For a number of years I was bothered by the fact I had no degree and at time's it was intimidating to me when I would sit and think about the people I was encountering in this work. Here I was working with highly educated people with medical degrees and MBA's. I often felt inadequate to speak in front of large audiences because I was not on the same educational level. When I would share these feelings with my wonderful wife, Jean, she would often remind me of how much God was using me to speak to people and motivate people to action, the ability to see hurting peoples and figure out ways to help them, and to see the outcome of a vision so that I could excite people to get behind that plan, be it medical people going or by others giving financially. In time that kind of encouragement from Jean and other close friends began to make me realize something important. It is not because of degrees that great things are accomplished. It is God who gives to us good things that we may accomplish great things.

A dear friend of mine is Jack Walker who is the Founding Director of Leadership Ministries Worldwide in Chattanooga, Tennessee. They print and distribute one of the best-produced bible study materials I have seen. They produce "The Preacher's Outline and Study Bible." Another one I like because it's for us Lay people to be able to teach from the New Testament in an easy to understand method is "The Teacher's Outline and Study Bible." Jean called my attention to a section of one study book on Galatians where part of an introduction said this: "Have you ever felt intimidated by someone who had more 'credentials' to serve than you did? They had all the 'right' papers, went to all the 'right' schools, and had been approved by all the 'right' agencies? Have you ever felt that you just did not measure up? If you have had these kinds of feelings, you are not alone. But rest assured the foundation of Christian service does not rest upon such man-made things as human credentials, schools, and papers of commendation. As helpful as these things may be, they are not the foundation of our service to Christ. The foundation for service is Christ and the great work He has called us to do."

Do I wish I had taken the time to get a degree? Yes I do! It could have helped me even more and I am thrilled my children went on to higher education but even with that they need something else. They need God to finish the work He began the day they chose to follow Christ. All of us can do great things as we allow God to work His plan for our lives. Philippians 1:6 says, "Being confident of this very thing, that he which has begun a good work in you will perform it until the day of Jesus Christ." God began a work in my life long ago and I am so pleased He chose to use me to bring and continue to bring healing to so many lives. If I can encourage anyone, it would be this: If you are in school, get all the tools you can through higher education. If you for whatever reason chose not to go on to higher education do not be discouraged. God has a plan and a purpose for each of us and all we have to do is allow Him to work that plan. His plan is for us to believe on His son, Jesus Christ. His plan is for us to love one another as He loved us and this means to care one for another. He will give you everything you need to accomplish this and the results for your life will be contentment and joy. Do we need anything else?

Publishers Note

The author has graciously decided to donate all royalties and further proceeds from *Created for Purpose* to Northwest Medical Teams International.